SEE YOU TONIGHT AND PROMISE TO BE A GOOD BOY!

WAR MEMORIES

SALO MULLER

Title: See You Tonight and Promise to Be a Good Boy! War Memories

Author: Salo Muller

ISBN 13: 9789492371560 (ebook)

ISBN 13: 9789492371553 (paperback)

© Uitgeverij Verbum and Salo Muller

Translation Mandy R. Evans-Wijnperle

Published by Amsterdam Publishers, The Netherlands, 2017

First published in the Netherlands in 2005 by Uitgeverij Houtekiet. Second and extended edition was published in 2014 by Uitgeverij Verbum as *Tot vanavond en lief zijn hoor!*

More information about the Verbum Holocaust Library can be found at verbum.nl.

For Conny

CONTENTS

PREFACE

After my parting words at my mother's funeral, or actually that of my aunt, a strange feeling came over me. I looked around. I was standing, with my wife and our two children, in the auditorium of the old Jewish cemetery at Muiderberg. My sister (my cousin) and her family, several other cousins and a few very dear friends and acquaintances were also present. So this was the remainder of my once large family.

As usual, my wife was standing right beside me. Alone. Yes, she was very much alone, without anyone there from her family. Her family did not exist any longer. She was the lonely remnant of her once large family.

We had become an appallingly small remainder that had to try to hold its own among the rest of the world's population. Maybe someday, by way of our children, this insignificant remainder may grow into a significant one again. This thought crossed my mind in what must have been the split second before the bier was rolled outside in the snow.

I dedicate this book to the man and woman who, through trial and error, raised me to become the person I am today. To you, Ju and Louis. Furthermore, I dedicate my book to my father, mother, uncles, aunts, cousins and my wife's family – to those who did not survive the gas chambers.

To my wife, Conny.

To my children and grandchildren: 'Lest they forget.'

And to everyone, who at the risk of losing their own life, dared to save mine.

I owe a great deal of gratitude to my wife, Conny. She spent many long evenings alone in our living room. But she never failed to support me in finishing this book.

And, of course, my thanks to Gerton van Boom who has supported me in word and deed as a friend and editor. Thanks to him my book has been renewed.

Salo Muller

INTRODUCTION

Murdered in Auschwitz

Each time I read the beginning of *Extinction* by Dr. J. Presser, shivers run up and down my spine. He writes: 'This book contains the history of a murder, premeditated mass murder on an unprecedented scale, executed in cold blood. The murderers were Germans, the victims were Jews.'

How was it possible that this deportation and the destruction that followed could have taken place? Who were these barbarians who had to answer for this? Didn't anyone try to stop this slaughter? Why didn't more Jews flee or hide? Six million people were cruelly killed. Murdered, gassed. Among those murdered were my parents. Yes, almost my entire large family, as well as my wife's family. I saved the letters from the Red Cross. They contain just one mere sentence: the name of my mother, Lena Blitz, born October 20th, 1908, deceased in Auschwitz February 12th, 1943. The other letter mentions my father's name in a similar manner: Louis Muller, born July 20th, 1903, deceased in Auschwitz April 30th, 1943.

I watched them standing on the stage of the Hollandsche

Schouwburg, high above my head. I was not allowed to join them. I screamed for my mother but I was not allowed to go to her. They took me to a daycare center across the street, where I cried for three days and three nights. I screamed and called for my parents but to no avail. I never saw them again. They were first transported to Westerbork in the Netherlands and shortly after to Auschwitz.

How could this possibly have happened?

To this day, I ask myself this same question over and over again. I try to suppress the anger and especially the overpowering grief that has taken a complete hold of me. Hardly a day goes by when I don't shed a tear but, unfortunately, it doesn't change a thing.

Still, one way or another I have to create order within myself. I'll have to find peace at last, without the aid of pills and endless discussions with medical professionals, without short-term intervention. I have read everything about this horrible drama. I read extensively.

But now the time has come to free myself of the story, my story, which is the story of my life. Will it do any good? Will it free me? I wonder, but I will have to rid myself of it at last.

I have not tried to put this story into a chronological order, except for dates that were of great importance. However, everything else I remember has received its place during the course of the story, the way I still remember it today, more than seventy years after this downfall.

1 PUSHED ASIDE BY THE WORLD

Thursday, October 29th, 1929. It was a date that would spell doom. The stock market in New York collapsed. Within a matter of hours innumerable investors lost all their money.

They were still rich when morning broke, but by evening they were left destitute. The international financial traffic and economic trade were in turmoil and money had lost its value completely. Construction companies and factories went bankrupt, stores closed their doors. For the masses, laborers and the middle class hard-pressed times had begun. The government introduced measures to curtail skyrocketing prices. This policy was brought about by what would later become a worldwide concept, known as 'the crash' or 'the crises'. Hundreds of thousands of people lost their job and had to go on welfare. Professor Lou de Jong would later write about this period: 'The massive unemployment during the thirties became the most important factor of the social truth and, during the German occupation, remained one of the most important aspects on the minds of many: a phantom that once it had reared its ugly head, it would remain in the awareness of the common man.'

Just to give an impression: in December of 1930 the Netherlands had

136.000 registered unemployed people. In 1933 their number had increased to a terrifying 380.000. Only 135.000 received any financial support. A year before the war broke out, the registered number of unemployed people was 406.000.

It is important for the *petit histoire* of my family to refer to this difficult time. The unemployed lived in isolation. Every day they tried to make ends meet. There was no money for anything. Even a newspaper was a luxury. Consequently, one hardly knew what was happening. Lou De Jong writes: 'Pushed aside by the world, they pushed the world aside.'

In spite of the massive unemployment and the threat of war, the daily fight for survival ruled most people's lives. No one could have guessed the seriousness of the situation, especially since the Dutch counted on their government to remain neutral again in the case of war.

In Germany political and social events followed each other in rapid succession. In November of 1918, German pacifists raised the flag of the republic over the rubble of the First World War. Emperor Wilhelm suffered a crushing defeat and fled to the neutral Netherlands. But Germany had also paid a heavy price: a 13% loss of territory, a ban on re-armament and international isolation. During the winter of 1918 / 1919 things started to go sour. Left- and rightwing extremists bombarded the shaky peace accords and created even greater confusion. Due to tactical considerations, the young German Communist Party availed itself of right-extremist objectives. One of its leaders began to bolster anti-Semitism, which was very much alive in circles on the right. On November 9th, 1923, Adolf Hitler sent the first jolt through the country. He staged a coup in Munich with the aid of his extremist stormtroopers. He was the first member of the so-called National Sozialistische Deutsche Arbeiterpartei (National Socialist Labor Party) or NSDAP.

Mr. De Jong would later comment about this still rather unknown figure: 'There is too little known about Hitler's youth, particularly his early years, to indicate the psychological background of this monomaniacal obsession, the need to dominate bordering on madness, this almost ceaseless delight in feelings of hatred; these traits were characteristic for his personality, as would become evident through his life and career.

There is no other way than that the rise of Hitler can be seen as the prelude to the tragedy of the Second World War and particularly the deliberate murder of millions of Jews. The facts of his life tell the story of the annihilation of ordinary people. Hitler was born on April 10th, 1889 in Braunau on the German-Austrian border. His father was the illegitimate child of Maria Ann Schicklgruber, a servant. A certain Johann Georg Hiedler acknowledged Aloïs Schicklgruber as his son and changed the name Hiedler to Hitler. At the age of 48, Aloïs remarried for the third time, this time to Klara Pölzl. Their fourth child was named Adolf. Three siblings born earlier had died; a little sister, named Paula, was yet to follow.

There is little known about Adolf Hitler's youth. His mother seems to have been a gentle woman. Young Hitler, however, was restless, short-tempered and stubborn. He dreamed of becoming a famous painter.

2 THE TOTAL ERADICATION OF THE JEWS

In 1905 Hitler experienced his very first blow – being rejected for painting and architecture classes at the Academy of Vienna. It disturbed him greatly. Nevertheless he stayed in the Austrian capital. It was here that the first signs of his true nature began to manifest themselves. He disliked his father, as well as ordinary people. Jews and anybody who was better off than he were no good in his opinion. He adored his mother. After she was diagnosed with cancer, the Jewish physician stayed with her until her last day on this earth. Hitler never spoke badly about him, quite the contrary!

In addition, he targeted the Austrian-Hungarian monarchy and hated Czechs, Slovaks and Croats. He left Vienna as 'an absolute anti-Semite, a mortal enemy of the Marxist worldview, but as a German chauvinist', as he himself admitted.

In February of 1914 the army rejected Hitler in Salzburg, even to work in the military assistance. Infuriated, he enrolled as a volunteer in Bavaria. He considered the defeat of Germany in the First World War unnecessary. He blamed the Jews, socialists, politicians and non-Germans and spelt out the charges in popular speeches and exhaustive arguments that would take him to the leadership of the

NSDAP. In 1919 he wrote in a memorandum: 'The reasonable anti-Semitism needs to start with the declassification of the Jews. The ultimate goal, however, should be indisputably the total eradication of the Jews.'

The coup staged in 1924 by Hitler and his cronies went up in smoke. Hitler ended up in prison where he wrote the first part of his life story and a political pogrom called *Mein Kampf,* with the help of his secretary, Rudolf Hess.

Five years later he was released from prison. He immediately demanded the leadership of the NSDAP, a growing movement with independent bodies of officials responsible for order and a Sturmabteilung, SA, under the leadership of Hermann Goering. Meanwhile in Germany in 1932, unemployment had reached six million, resulting in poverty, disorder and an incredible devaluation of the German mark. The norms of a rational society evaporated. That's why it was possible for the old Chancellor Von Hindenburg to appoint the emerging nationalist leader, Hitler, as his successor. This happened on January 31st, 1933.

The conservatives in the Reichstag, the German parliament, did not succeed in stopping Hitler. Hitler would not stand for half measures and directed Germany towards the abyss. He immediately had concentration camps built, where his political opponents, critical journalists and union members disappeared. Disappeared for good.

German society experienced a speedy metamorphosis and sank into a puddle of terror and fear. In the meantime, the Nazi party knew how to bring the admiration for the Führer to great heights. They gave the already dissatisfied people a sense of false hope.

The majority of the Germans sought refuge in their new leader. Hitler gave jobs to millions who were unemployed in the arms industry and the construction of highways, so that the army divisions that were being set up could move quickly. In 1933, a highly-regulated Germany had only six army divisions. In 1939, at the start of the

Second World War, 51 rolled and marched along the Autobahn! Meanwhile, Hitler took his power and influence across old borders. In 1935 he took away the buffer neutrality of the Saarland, which had been enforced by the Treaty of Versailles. In 1936 he occupied the Rhineland. In 1937 and 1938 he had his eye on his native country, Austria, bringing about the Anschluss (the annexation of Austria). After that he gave full rein to his aggression towards Czechoslovakia and the Sudetenland. On September 3rd, 1939, Hitler invaded Poland. A few hours later Poland, England and France officially declared war on Germany.

In the Netherlands there was disbelief. The Dutch hoped that their so cherished neutral status would keep them out of this global conflict. After all, the last real hostilities on Dutch soil dated back to the Duke of Alba, the Spanish inquisitor of the 16th century and the archenemy of William of Orange. Therefore, the term 'war' was unknown to modern the Netherlands, contrary to their neighboring countries.

At first the Dutch newspapers paid plenty of attention to Hitler's takeover. They followed the evolution in Germany with increasing concern. Later on, strangely enough, they proceeded to act as though nothing had happened, as if they thought that things would turn out better than expected.

That was also the case for most of the Jews in the Netherlands. The author Geert Mak writes in his book *Amsterdam: A Brief Life of the City*: 'Even the Jews, who had lived here peacefully for generations, could not imagine that it was that bad in Germany.'

It is a fact that many citizens of the Netherlands were not aware of what had happened in the thirties. As an example, in September of 1935 the German Reichstag had unanimously adopted the Nuremberg Laws, containing a number of anti-Jewish provisions. Laws that would change the everyday life for millions.

For one, Jews were no longer allowed to marry non-Jews and Jews were no longer allowed to hire non-Jewish domestic servants. Citizenship was taken away from them; they were no longer fellow citizens. They were no longer considered human beings. They became nobodies: 'Untermenschen'.

It all happened very fast. Men were forced to write the name Israel before their own name on all their documents and the women Sarah. That way the authorities would immediately know that they were dealing with Jews.

Signs appeared everywhere with the words: 'No Jews allowed'. The first appeared in 1936: the year I was born. Only a few years later, all of those laws and prohibitions would be indiscriminately adopted in the Netherlands as well.

November 10th, 1938 should not be allowed to ever be erased from memory. That's when the first pogrom took place, organized by the government. It is now known as the Kristallnacht. Synagogues were burned down. Stores and homes were destroyed, and Jewish men arrested and deported to concentration camps. 92 Jewish men were murdered. This has been described in a painful and distressing way in *Confrontation with Destiny*, a deposition detailing these events by my friend Werner Bloch.

3 JEWISH AMSTERDAM

How did the Netherlands, and especially Amsterdam since this was the city where most of the Jews lived, cope during this period? Around 1940 our country counted approximately 140.000 Jews that were either members of a Jewish community or a religious organization. Approximately 80.000 Jews resided in the capital and of these more than 10.000 were not Dutch nationals. The makeup of the Jewish communities was diverse. Jews of Spanish and Portuguese descent (Sephardic) were mainly living in Amsterdam, while German and East European Jews (Ashkenazi), descendants of Jews who had fled to the Netherlands in the 17th century, were spread out across the country. In 1796 the National Assembly acknowledged all Jews living in our country as Dutch citizens. To mark this merger, a census taken in 1797 showed approximately 20.000 Ashkenazi and 2.800 Portuguese Jews in a total population of 200.000. These Jews had been living peacefully in our country for generations. The Dutch government had never drawn a line between Jews and non-Jews. This would only come about when the so-called mandatory 'Declaration of Aryan origin' was brought into existence by the occupying forces.

Social changes followed at a very slow pace. Many Jews in

Amsterdam were living on welfare, and had settled in the neighborhood of Waterlooplein, a mixed area of Jews and non-Jews. Increasingly more Jews became interested in the medical profession, the legal profession and journalism, but the majority still lived in poverty. A cultural change also became noticeable when Jewish schools replaced Yiddish with Dutch. Steadily more and more Jews left for municipal schools for the poor. The government gave this development its full support, thinking that it would speed up integration. After 1850 Dutch became the accepted language for Amsterdam Jews, even though many Yiddish words and expressions remain part of the everyday spoken language to this day.

Due to changes in the world of business and the expansion of trade, a large number of Jews were able to further themselves to become important businessmen. For example, Asscher, a leading company in the diamond trade, was able to put hundreds of diamond cutters to work, allowing them to earn a proper living. And a small dry goods store located at de Nieuwendijk called de Bijenkorf grew into a large chain that still carries the same name today. Enterprising Jews dominated the textile industry and the antiques business. But still only a small portion of Jewish citizens was offered opportunities. As a result their lives improved very slowly. In 1914 more than half of the Jews in Amsterdam were working in the diamond industry. Outside of their religious communities they had started to become involved in the social welfare of the Jews. It appeared that the distance between Jews and non-Jews was getting progressively smaller. Consequently, interracial marriages were on the up and the majority of Jews in the capital felt foremost like citizens of Amsterdam, or Amsterdammers as they're known to the general public. This was undoubtedly the situation until 1940. One felt safe in one's own city, in neutral Holland. What could possibly happen to us?

Jews listened with a sympathetic ear to the stories of Jewish and other refugees from Germany and Austria, but overall these tales were taken with a grain of salt and received with skepticism. Exaggerated, they'd say! Could it really be as dangerous as they claimed? This mentality may have contributed to the fact that the percentage of Dutch Jews murdered by the Germans was the highest of any west European country.

When 1940 rolled around, it became apparent that the Jews as well as the rest of the Dutch citizens were totally unprepared for a German attack.

To paint a picture of the prewar coexistence between Jews and non-Jews in the Netherlands I need to mention the Nationaal Socialistische Beweging founded by Anton Mussert, an engineer with the Provincial Ministry of Transport and Public Works. His program capitalized on the massive unemployment and poverty, taking a page from Hitler's book. At the time of the provincial state elections in 1935 his party, the NSB, obtained as many as 44 seats. As a result 50.000 Dutch citizens were swayed to become members.

Still, there were those who warned against the dangerous conduct of the NSB, which resulted in the loss of half of their seats at the next election to the Dutch parliament.

May 10th, 1940. A crucial moment in our history. The Germans attacked their neighboring countries on the western borders. The Netherlands, Belgium, Luxembourg and France met with defeat. A secret report later showed that the attack had been prepared as early as in 1939. In the early days of the war, the 105 French, 9 British, 22 Belgian and 10 Dutch divisions were facing 136 German divisions. They were no match for the German war machine.

4 THE FLIGHT OF QUEEN WILHELMINA

I believe that the flight of Queen Wilhelmina and a number of her ministers to England contributed to the fact that our country was immediately overrun. At the time of her installation in 1898, she had talked about 'her calling, her life's task and duty and that the House of Orange would never, no, never be able to do enough for the Netherlands'. Did she indeed do everything within her power to protect and help her Jewish citizens? I hope that it will become clear from my story that it was only a handful of individuals that helped the Jews. However, I would still like to mention the following about Wilhelmina: she was strong, temperamental, intelligent and maybe 'courageous'. She was an only child, who had been through a strict upbringing surrounded by governesses. Once she became queen, her life turned into nothing but protocol. Openly addressing her was not allowed, not to mention disagreeing with her. She was deeply religious, with the Bible as her support and refuge. From her mother's as well as her father's side she became very well acquainted with Germany and the Germans. Furthermore, she often visited Germany.

Again, I would like to quote Lou de Jong: 'The constitutional king is entirely authorized, within the boundaries of the ministerial responsibilities to exert his influence. He may be or become a puppet but he is not forced to. Neither a single bill, nor a single royal decree needs his automatic signature. He may either raise objections or urge for reconsideration. Besides other privileges, there is the privilege to be consulted.'

In 1938 Queen Wilhelmina put pressure on Prime Minister Hendrikus Colijn. She insisted on strengthening the country's defense, but Colijn ignored her. Wilhelmina called this refusal irresponsible. The constant differences of opinion on this subject were rarely, if ever, brought out into the open. In this case the queen would turn out to be right. Four days after the Germans crossed the border, the Netherlands had to give up the fight. The army was ill-equipped to withstand invasion.

The armament did not start until 1937, which was much too late because at that point suppliers were no longer able to deliver what the Dutch army needed. The air force did not amount to much with only 104 planes, of which only 52 were modern ones. The Germans destroyed part of this fleet almost immediately. Tanks and anti-aircraft artillery were highly inadequate and to top it all off there was the departure of the royal family to England. On May 12th, 1940 under pressure from Queen Wilhelmina, Princess Juliana left. At first she was accompanied by Prince Bernhard, who was an officer in active service and whose wish it was to stay in the Netherlands. He would indeed quickly return because what kind of shameful impression would he have made he had he gone to England to take his wife and children out of harm's way while the country was at war? In the armed forces one could not take one's family into consideration.

I like to point out that this would have been the day on which the Jews should have realized that maybe they should also start thinking about their safety. But they were not advised to do so, not even by their queen. If the royal family didn't deem it safe any longer, could they not have realized what was in store for the Jews? Especially after what they had learned about the events taking place in Germany. The royals' despair was evident in the futile telegrams for help that the queen tried to send to friendly monarchies and internationally influential individuals.

Concerning her departure, Lou de Jong writes: 'Stay and become captured? Never! Did Willem de Zwijger wait for the arrival of Alba? Was Hitler not the same demonic figure as this Spanish tyrant? Queen Wilhelmina herself noted: "It did not make any sense to allow myself being captured and sent to Berlin, separated from my people. In such case, I would not have been able to do anything at all. So I had to leave."'

In regard to this, a board of inquiry would later conclude 'that the Government Policy '40-'45 of the House of Commons, taken on May 13th, 1940 at the Hoek van Holland to move the seat of Government to England, had been one of the most important decisions of the entire war era'.

In my estimation this was an extremely exaggerated and a truly absurd conclusion. The queen, without consulting her ministers in any way, just fled to England. And I would like to call to mind her oath! Should it not have been her duty to support the troops, so her citizens would have understood that she was not going to give in to the demands of the wicked occupiers? Neither the troops nor the citizens were aware of her departure, let alone were there words of warning from the queen and her ministers from which the Jewish citizens could have concluded that their lives might be in danger, and not to expect any help from their own government. The authorities that were left behind would not hinder the Germans from doing what they pleased!

We have now come to realize what the consequences were going to be for millions of people.

The invasion itself on May 10th, 1940, despite the strategically best positioning of our troops, could only lead to a quick capitulation, notwithstanding the Grebbelinie, de Oud-Hollandse Waterlinie, de Betuwe, Maas and Waal rivers, de Peel and a few divisions in the west. In addition we had to combat the German collaborators, the so-called fifth column. We would later find out that the Germans had threatened to release paratroops to imprison the royal family, ministers and high-ranking military personnel.

What had happened in those few days of trying to stand up for ourselves? 2.500 soldiers had been killed, as well as many citizens, and hundreds had tried to commit suicide. On May 14th, a bright, sunny day, the Germans broke through near Rotterdam and bombed the city, killing hundreds of people. When they threatened to flatten Utrecht and other cities as well, General Winkelman was left no other choice than to surrender.

5   A TALK WITH HITLER?

In the meantime Belgium had also surrendered and not quite a month later Paris was conquered. Contrary to his actions in France, however, Hitler decided to release our prisoners of war. It seemed like a generous act, but soon he would demonstrate his cruelty to the Russian soldiers, who were murdered and starved to death by the thousands. He put a new person in charge of the Netherlands, Dr. Arthur Seyss-Inquart, a member of the German government, with the official and pretentious title of 'State Commissioner of the Dutch Occupied Territories'. This Austrian lawyer had previously played a not so nice part in the annexation of Austria in March of 1938. Seyss-Inquart moved with his family to The Hague and initially governed the country using appropriated Dutch channels. However, the Germans were the ones who made the decisions. They checked everything, gave the orders but left the implementation to our authorities.

Again, there was the question of how to deal with it all. Should all orders be indiscriminately carried out? Would it be possible to negotiate with this man, Hitler? By now it was known that he ignored international laws.

Professor Mr. Robert Regout was one of the first ones to point out that there were applicable international laws in one of his articles. In the end, he had to pay for it with his life. Following a journey through several prisons, he died in the hell of Dachau.

During those difficult times, the business world tried to maintain and continue its activities as well as it knew how. As a result, one could not expect any protests or action from them. On the contrary, they accepted military orders from the Germans.

How did the Jews react to this chaotic situation? In the early stages of the occupation the fear hit home. They realized that the anti-Semitism of Hitler would become a vital issue. On the other hand, however, they allowed themselves to be appeased. For instance, in an article in *Het Nieuw Israelitisch Weekblad* (1938) with a circulation of 15.000 copies the author insisted that 'not everything about Nazism was to be condemned'. Did this mean that there was no reason to be afraid, maybe?

Could they possibly not have been aware of Hitler's address to the Reichstag on January 30th, 1939 concerning the extermination of the Jews? The text reads: 'The Jewish people must be exterminated. Himmler must carry it out.' People must have heard about it, but they did not comprehend its true meaning and significance.

In the fall of 1940 the Netherlands began to recognize, for the very first time, a distinction between Jews and non-Jews. On October 18th, all public officials received a form that they needed to complete before October 26th. Are you Aryan or non-Aryan? Ancestry needed to be carefully investigated. Do you have Jewish ancestors? This piece of paper was dutifully signed by the Jews, afraid of consequences. Regret would follow!

The Amsterdam Lyceum, the school that I would be attending for three years after the war, never signed this 'Declaration of Aryan Origin'. This was an exception!

6 ROUNDUPS

In January of 1941 the Germans began to step up their actions. All Jewish government officials were fired. They unveiled their plan to drive the Jews out of The Hague and the coastal area. Ritual slaughter was forbidden. The Joodse Raad (Jewish Council) came into being, a hideous institution. The Germans provoked anti-Semitic street riots in Amsterdam, kicked off by the NSB. This intensified the resistance from Jewish assault groups, but the Germans could count on a lot of support from the followers of the new order, and the NSB and its cronies.

In addition the Germans organized a huge riot in Amsterdam and arrested numerous defenseless Jewish people, among them my parents. That's when it really began. In the course of 1941 the Germans robbed the Jews of all their possessions, not only those pertaining to their business, but real estate and other belongings as well. To any Jewish business they appointed a manager, a so-called *Verwalter*. In addition, Amsterdam now had its own Jewish quarter and public notices that read 'No Jews allowed' appeared everywhere. Jews were only to receive services from Jewish doctors, pharmacists, lawyers and teachers. They were no longer allowed in movie theaters, restaurants, the zoo, parks, swimming pools, sports, playing or athletic fields, museums and other public buildings. As of September, 1941, Jewish children were only permitted to attend Jewish schools. All these changes happened in rapid succession. Life had turned into a hell!

Still, there were a lot of people who believed that the war would soon pass. They were under the assumption that Hitler and his cronies could not continue this way, but meanwhile the Jews were left to fend for themselves. The government offered no protection and they grew to endure the discrimination against the Jews. You could summarize the mood of the Jews in a few words: they were afraid, shortsighted and submissive. They acted like sheep without the slightest hint of protest. The orders of the occupiers were carefully passed on by the Jewish Council to the person or persons concerned.

At the end of 1941 all unemployed Jews were facing the camps. The Jewish Council advised Jews to register and definitely not try to steer clear of attention. *Het Joodsche Weekblad* also published these instructions, which intimidated many.

The ordinances to isolate the Jews were issued in stages. It all began on May 2nd, 1942 with the Star of David, which all Jews had to wear on their outer garments for immediate recognition. Because of this action their freedom of movement, or whatever was left of it, became very restricted. On June 30th, 1942 another heartless verdict was issued: Jews were no longer allowed to make use of trains, streetcars, bicycles, taxicabs or public telephones. It seems incomprehensible that someone can come up with something like this to eliminate a group of fellow citizens and countrymen without anyone rebelling against it. But it happened. And the Germans were not yet finished.

Jews were no longer allowed to pay visits to non-Jews, nor enter their homes. A curfew was instated from 8 p.m. till 6 a.m. Even Jewish doctors were no longer allowed to go out to care for their patients during these hours. It goes without saying that these actions became the talk of the town. One couldn't think of anything else. What to do next?

7 BORN ON A LEAP DAY

I was born on February 29th, 1936 – a leap year – at home on Molenbeekstraat 34 in Amsterdam. I enjoyed wonderful preschool years, with great birthdays; everyone spoiled me.

It was a house filled with family and friends, grandmas, grandpas, aunts, uncles and cousins. I was terribly spoiled by everyone. Even though my parents cherished their Jewish identity, they definitely didn't come across as being orthodox. Every Saturday morning I went with Grandpa Barend Muller to Sjoel. He was a cantor in the then famous choir of Engelander, where he had discovered his love for music. On my fourth birthday he gave me a small drum set with beautiful, shiny drums. Whenever I had a chance I would play them, which meant almost every moment of the day.

My parents were employed by De Vries van Buuren, a well-known textile wholesale firm in Amsterdam. My father was the purchaser of the socks and stockings department while my mother worked in the sales department. Time moved along without complications, or so it seemed. I was an affectionate and sweet little boy, who was very satisfied with his life. I knew exactly when my dad was coming home from work as he always whistled a particular opera jingle when he turned the corner of our street. What a wonderful moment it was! I even heard the tune in my sleep. My parents really spoiled me and buried me under a mountain of toys. In addition, I had my own beautiful room that looked out on our street. Our home carried the signature of the well-known interior designer Bueno de Mesquita, who had drawn up and arranged everything with my mother. Beautiful pictures of beach scenes and seascapes adorned our walls. I specifically remember the organized manner in which my toys were put away. There were the balls, the toy trains, the toy cars and especially the books. I devoured them, especially my *Winnie-the-Pooh*. Every evening I would look at the pictures and my father and mother would read to me. It was the highlight of my day.

Our family and our extended family were very close. We would visit each other every Saturday, either at the home of my father's parents in Lepelstraat or at the home of my grandmother in Blasiusstraat, where she ran a small store. A plaque above the door of the store had a wonderful message that read: 'He who is willing to sacrifice will achieve'. It was the very first sentence I learned to read! But my carefree youth ended abruptly.

Even though my family, for the sake of my grandparents, lived a conservative lifestyle, we suddenly began to listen to the radio on Saturdays. We bought newspapers from which the news was read out loud. We yelled, made a lot of telephone calls and hardly got out of the house anymore, not even to visit grandma and grandpa. There was often whispering about things not intended for a child's ears. Thankfully, the daily visits that I enjoyed so much continued. I loved people and liked to sit on their lap and relished the times when they played games with me. They always insisted I do a drum solo for them. I seemed to notice, however, that they did not really come for me but for something else. They signed papers, listened to the radio and at times cried together.

When evening fell, the curtains were carefully drawn. I didn't like it; it made the room so dark.

I attended kindergarten at Victorieplein. Every morning, either my father or my mother would take me to school. I just wanted to love everybody and had my own circle of friends. And I still remember a beautiful girl named Roosje. Her mother and my mother were best friends. She now lives in the United States with her husband, children and grandchildren.

This idyllic period was rudely disturbed. I entered a chapter of my life that I would carry with me forever and that I can never forget. I remember exactly how it all began...

8 A SUNNY DAY IN MAY

It was a sunny day in May and my mother was walking me to school. It promised to be a hot day, despite the season, and I didn't have to wear a big coat or hat. When we reached the school I left her with one last big hug and ran inside. 'See you tonight, and promise to be a good boy!' she called after me. Then she took the streetcar to her job at De Vries van Buuren in Jodenbreestraat.

At one point during class, Mr. Colthof, our upstairs neighbor, came to get me. He was wearing a very nice gray suit with a small red handkerchief in his breast pocket. He seemed a bit uneasy. At first he tried to carry me but pretty soon he put me down. Holding his hand tightly we continued to walk, which seemed more like running to keep up with his long strides. Mr. Colthof kept touching his red handkerchief.

I noticed that his thumb had started to bleed. He had cut himself on a small pair of scissors that were hidden behind the handkerchief in his breast pocket. His thumb bled badly enough for us to have to go to a pharmacy to buy a roll of bandage. When he was finished wrapping the bandage around his thumb I had to press my finger on it to help him shape a nice bow.

We continued walking, passing our home, until we reached the home of my aunt and uncle at Dintelstraat 47. My mother and I visited them almost every day, so I didn't think anything of it that Mr. Colthof was taking me to Aunt Ju, my mother's sister. Mr. Colthof kept rubbing his bold head. By now, the bandage had turned very red from the blood. There was even blood on his head. To me, it was all pretty exciting, I would have so much to tell mom and dad that night when they would put me to bed! When we finally arrived at Aunt Ju and Uncle Louis's, everyone was crying.

What had happened? The Nazis had taken charge in a most brutal way. During a massive raid, the Jewish employees of De Vries van Buuren had not been spared. In the morning they had come with two police vans to take people away. Among them was my mother. My dad happened to have taken a day off, but he soon learned through the grapevine that my mother had been arrested and taken to the Hollandsche Schouwburg at Plantage Middenlaan. It was here that the Nazis had improvised a holding pen to temporarily corral any Jews who had been arrested. My father immediately realized the seriousness of the situation and, without delay, he packed a suitcase with all kinds of stuff and rushed out to find my mother. He also asked Mr. Colthof to get me out of school and to take me to the Hollandsche Schouwburg. When Mr. Colthof left my aunt and uncle, there was a deafening silence. Aunt Ju cried silently and Uncle Louis didn't say a word.

I felt afraid, even though I didn't quite understand what was going on. My father and mother still hadn't returned. What was keeping them so long?

Suddenly the doorbell rang. The shrill, piercing sound severed the silence. My uncle and aunt were noticeably terrified while my little cousin, Etty, continued sleeping peacefully in her little bed. I was told to stand behind the door of the living room, not to speak another word and above all not to move. Aunt Ju quickly went to lie down on the bed while Uncle Louis answered the door.

Three men dressed in black barged in. They had come to arrest all of us. Aunt Ju began waving around a doctor's certificate. Impossible! She had suffered a miscarriage and her husband had to take care of her. Besides, little Etty was not allowed outside, she had scarlet fever, extremely contagious! The men began a loud discussion. When they were ready to leave empty-handed, I did a very dumb thing. I crawled out from behind the door. Silence, absolute silence! What had I done?

'Whose child is that? You're telling us he's not your son? Then he has to come with us. Hurry up!'

I was carried downstairs and thrown in the back of a waiting truck. Inside the truck a bunch of seated and standing people received me. I was trembling with fear, but at the same time I felt a sense of excitement. Could it be possible that they were taking me to mom and dad? More and more people were being pushed into the truck. When there was no more room, we left. It was a short trip. We stopped in the middle of the road near a large building. 'De Schouwburg,' I heard people say. Most people jumped off the truck, but some of them fell to the ground. I was lifted, none too softly, from the cargo area.

Inside the building hundreds of people were milling around. We were taken to a large hall and that's where, at last, I saw them, mom and dad, high above my head and completely out of reach. They were standing on the stage between suitcases and blanket rolls. Many people were crying. I ran towards the stage and tried to climb up on it but a soldier blocked my path. I did not understand what his shouting was all about, but I did understand that he tried to prevent me from going to my parents. They kept waving at me and even blew me kisses. That's when I started to scream.

9 THE LAST TIME I SAW MY PARENTS

My screams were so piercing, so penetrating that everybody in the large hall fell silent. I kept crying out for my father and mother, but there was nothing anyone could do. A strange man pulled me away from the stage, and I tried desperately to fight back. I caught a final glance from my father and mother. I never saw them again.

Alex Bakker wrote in his book *Dag pap, tot morgen: Joodse kinderen gered uit de crèche*: 'Salo Muller's parents, Louis Muller and Lena Blitz, were deported from Amsterdam to Westerbork on Saturday November 28th, 1942, where they were housed in barrack 65. On Tuesday February 9th they were deported to Auschwitz, where Lena Blitz was murdered on Friday February 12th, 1943. Louis was admitted to the camp to work and was finally murdered on Friday the 30th of April, 1943. Salo Muller survived the war by going into hiding.'

The man pushed me forcibly onto the street and handed me over to a nurse, wearing a white and blue dress and oversized glasses. She picked me up and took me to a house across the street where, on the second floor, I was put in a wooden crib, clothed and all. I continued crying and screaming, kicking and hitting. 'Papa and Mama have to come.' I kept calling for my parents but they did not come, they never returned. I learned much later that I had kept this up for four long days.

After four days yet another stranger came to get me. 'Please don't cry,' he said. 'Uncle Louis is here and you may go with him.' The man lifted me onto his shoulders and carried me down the stairs. At the bottom of the stairs I saw my sweet, tall Uncle Louis, at that moment, for me, a most wondrous sight. I calmed down. We walked towards him and when I was put down I ran to him. Without uttering a word he grabbed my hand and we walked away as quickly as possible.

After a long walk we finally ended up at Dintelstraat 47 again. Aunt Ju's greeting was very emotional and as she was crying I became completely soaked from the kisses under which she buried me. Through her tears she called me a big boy and a sweet boy and told me that she was very proud of me for being so brave.

While I was out of daycare, I wasn't taken off the paperwork. Süskind, the director of the Hollandsche Schouwburg and the daycare, thought that was best. And that's how I ended up on his list of children. He saved hundreds of children from the hands of the Germans this way.

Life went on. Aunt Ju was often gone. She went to see the folks at the Jewish Council to find out the latest news. She often cried and all that time I was beside myself that my parents would not be returning. Where did they go? Without me?

At some point a yellow star was sewn onto my blue coat. Everyone had to get such a star anyway. I really liked it and showed it proudly to everyone I met.

One evening, after we had finished our dinner, Aunt Ju started to pack a small suitcase. She filled it with my clothes, my wooden rabbit and some candies. I was hoping that she would take me to my father and mother, but it was not so.

Moments later a stranger walked into the living room. 'This is Uncle

Co,' Aunt Ju introduced him. 'Go ahead, you may shake his hand.' I did, but then a disaster ensued. I heard them say that this Uncle Co was going to take me with him. He was working for VAMI, an ice-cream and milk factory. I would get delicious popsicles, as many as I wanted. 'Those are the ones you like so much, right?' Fear began to take a hold of me and I started to cry. Uncle Co, however, was tall and strong. He lifted me off the floor and carried me downstairs.

He was living somewhere in east Amsterdam in an upper-story apartment. A dark, small place. He introduced his wife to me: Aunt Marie. I had to shake hands with a stranger again, when my mama had told me to never shake hands with a stranger. To distract me, Uncle Co took me upstairs to the roof. That's where he kept his pigeons. I didn't care about them at all. I just wanted one thing: to go home.

10   MY FIRST HIDING PLACE

It took quite a while before I understood that this was my first hiding place. It was also the beginning of my many wanderings through the Netherlands, which would not end until 1946.

In the interim, how were the Jews in general doing? What was their situation like in Europe? During the infamous Reichskristallnacht of 1938 Jews in Germany were mistreated and arrested. Synagogues went up in flames. Homes were ransacked and destroyed. A hate campaign against the Jews had begun. There were two kinds of policemen, one that was willing to come to their aid, albeit on a small scale, and another that took part in the hate campaigns and did not refrain from lending a helping hand with the destruction and plunder.

The Nazis kept themselves hidden behind Jewish organizations, which were called in to assist. For a brief moment it looked as if there was a glimmer of hope when there was talk about a so-called emigration of Jews. It appeared impossible, however, to cleanse the various regions of the millions of Jews that way. Still, the Nazis wanted to get rid of them at any cost. In 1940 the Madagascar Plan was developed, which meant that all Jews would be isolated on this island, a sort of reservation, allowing for approximately four million people. Naturally it would be under the supervision of the Germans. That plan was, of course, unachievable. All that remained was 'evacuation', which simply meant extermination. The German agency that occupied itself specifically with extermination was Referat IVB4 of the Reichssicherheitshauptamt (the Reich Security Main Office). Heading this agency was Eichmann, who appointed Müller as the person in charge.

When, during the night of May 10th, 1940, the German army crossed the Dutch border, genuine panic broke out among the Jews. They now clearly understood the tragic fate of the Jews in Germany and that nothing was being done about it. Hence, what was one to expect in Holland?

A few fled to the south, to Belgium, France, Spain or Portugal, and some were able to escape to the United States and even further away than that. The majority, however, stayed at home. In those early days of May, a number of Jewish citizens had suddenly rushed to the coast, to the city of IJmuiden, from where they tried to escape to England on whatever ship was available, only to watch the last ships leave without them, their attempts crushed. Some had paid large amounts of money for a ticket but all there was left for them to do was watch. This failed small-scale odyssey would later be referred to as 'the tragedy of IJmuiden', an event that caused even the authorities to panic. Even my aunt and uncle tried to board a ship to England, but unfortunately there was no space for them either.

Most Jews stayed in Amsterdam. Why or rather what for? Many were afraid and didn't want to leave without their parents. Then there was the lack of money and the need for transportation or just not wanting to leave Holland. People still hoped that the dark skies would brighten again.

All the same, a wave of suicides followed. Whole families and their extended families turned on the gas tap. Others overdosed on Veronal first before surrendering themselves to this fate. Suicides by hanging, self-inflicted gun shots, the cutting of wrists and through the use of morphine all took place. It was like a horrifying epidemic.

In the meantime, the mayor of Amsterdam, Dr. W. de Vught, tried to appease the Jews by telling them that the German military commander had assured him that the Jews in the Netherlands would not be harmed. The new governor of the Netherlands, Seyss-Inquart, kept quiet and only a year later expressed himself concerning the Jews.

11 THE ARTERY CUT AND THE BLOOD DRAINED OUT OF ME

It was not only in our corner of Europe that the Nazis began to prepare for the eradication of the Jews. In eastern Europe their gruesome practices took on dramatic proportions. In June of 1941, Hitler crossed the border into the Soviet Union. Special battalions immediately followed the Wehrmacht, their only order being to kill Jewish people. These Einsatzkommandos killed more than one million Jews in Poland, the Baltic and Russia as they followed the troops. In order to speed up and simplify this large-scale extinction, they called on Eichmann. He had gas chambers built in Poland, in cities such as Chelmo, Treblinka, Sobibor, Belsec, Majdanek and Auschwitz-Birkenau, and in early 1942, under a veil of secrecy, the first transports of Polish Jews to these camps were being planned. To the public, these matters were spoken about in code, with phrases such as 'the Jewish problem' or 'the relocation of the Jews'.

In the Netherlands, Jews became involved in the resistance, risking their own lives. We never experienced anything like the ghetto uprising in Warsaw; the fear of being arrested and sentenced to death as a result of overt resistance was too great. Thus the general opinion was that the Jews were scaredy-cats who voluntarily allowed themselves to be slaughtered.

The first assault group consisted solely of Jews, which, under the leadership of the boxer Joop Cosman, became the most notorious one. Through his boxing school he gathered a group of about forty well-trained young men. They only acted when absolutely necessary. Of the 140.000 Jews only a few hundred joined the resistance. Of the total Dutch citizenry, the number was a mere few thousand.

There was, however, a militant organization, the Institution to Defend the Cultural and Social Rights of the Jews (SRJ). Founded in Amsterdam, its main goal was to strengthen the fighting spirit of the young people. However, it did not succeed in supplying its members with weapons. In this context it's important to remember that the first order enforced on the Jewish Council by the occupier, on January 12th, 1941, was the surrender of weapons. No weapons were surrendered.

On February 11th a horrible incident occurred. A member of the NSB, named Koot, provoked the residents of the Jewish quarter to a fight. The young men who were part of the commando group beat him up so badly that he died a few days later. The Germans described it thus: 'In Amsterdam a member of the NSB was beaten to death. A Jew had come up from behind him and cut his main artery, whereupon he sucked his blood.' This incident foreshadowed a tragedy.

On February 19th, in Van Wouwstraat in Amsterdam, Cosman's commandos clashed with a team from the Sicherheitspolizei. The fight took place in the ice-cream parlor of the Jewish immigrants Cahn and Kohn. The consequences were disastrous: 425 Jewish men, both older and young men between 18 and 35, were arrested and vanished to the concentration camps.

But that was not the end of it. During an unexpected roundup on Saturday afternoon, February 22th, in Jonas Daniel Meijerplein, the heart of the Jewish district, more men and boys were arrested. The next day the same thing occurred, but this time many non-Jewish residents of Amsterdam were present to witness the events. It was largely the Communist Party that protested. A year later, two of their leaders would be shot to death. Workers from the municipal services and the public transport network and shop owners went on strike the next day. Using pamphlets, they made clear that they were demanding the release of the Jewish prisoners. They also wanted Jewish children to be exempt from the Nazi violence and called for families to take them in.

Some Amsterdam residents were on the side of their Jewish fellow citizens and opposed the actions carried out by the Germans. They felt that something needed to be done. After the brawl in the ice-cream parlor and the ensuing arrests, their tolerance had reached its limit and a call went out for a general strike. The first ones to respond were the workers of the city's sanitation department. Streetcars and buses did not leave their stations and traffic came to a complete standstill. The people protested fiercely against the occupier. The event became known as the February Strike.

The *Dockworker* statue by Mari Andriessen on Jonas Daniel Meijerplein not only serves as a constant reminder of that time but also keeps the memories alive of those who lost the battle.

The Germans struck back mercilessly. German troops shot people at random in the streets. One of the owners of the ice-cream parlor, Ernst Cahn, was executed.

Cities and smaller towns that had the courage to join the strike, such as Weesp, Hilversum, Zaandam, Wormerveer, Muiden, Huizen and Utrecht, paid a heavy price.

Many civil servants were fired. The new man in charge of Noord-Holland, General Friedrich Christiansen, signed off on these measures. Despite the fact that even churches joined the protests, it became very difficult for small resistance groups to find new people who had the courage to join the movement. In the end, 700 Catholics of Jewish descent were arrested and sent to Auschwitz via Westerbork.

In Amsterdam itself, the resistance continued its work on a smaller scale. They got the guards of the Hollandsche Schouwburg drunk and smuggled a few people out to escape death.

Many children were pulled away from their parents and a number of Jews were smuggled successfully across the border. One would still meet Jews in some form of resistance, only there were fewer and fewer as time went on.

12 INSPECTION OF THE BARE BUMS

Suspicion became fact: my father and mother would never return. They had been transported to Auschwitz via Westerbork. There was no word about the whereabouts of Aunt Ju, Uncle Louis and my cousin Etty. After the war I found a letter from my parents. It was sent on February 9th, 1943. The letter was addressed to the family B.L. Muller, Lepelstaat 14 in Amsterdam. B. Muller was my grandfather Barend, the person who I was named after. The sender was Bornstein, Barak 65, Lager Westerbork. I thought, and still do, the content of the letter was unbearable.

'Today (9-2-1943) we will be transported. Everyone in their turn. Everything will continue. We have survived for 10 weeks and are very brave. Will you pass on our greetings to everyone and stay strong. We will thank God when we see you again soon.

Many thanks for everything that you've done for us and all the best to everyone.

Kisses for Pietersen and mother as well. Goodbye.

Lena and Louis Bornstein.'

I think my father meant to address me when he mentioned 'Pietersen'.

From the documentation at Westerbork it appeared that I had also spent ten weeks there together with my father and mother. On paper, I was deported to Westerbork along with my parents. According to the Germans, I was there. That list was composed by Süskind. It was a courageous gesture, and part of the reason I survived the war.

On February 5th my father wrote another letter to his sister in Biesboschstraat 28 H in Amsterdam: 'Mail received. Thanks.' It is addressed to the family Berghoff-Mazzeltof and the senders are Lena and Louis Muller, Barak 65 Westerbork. The 'Mazzeltof' was a response to the mail they had received. The family Berghoff had somehow secured a 'sper' or a deferment. They stayed out of the hands of the Germans. Luckily they survived the war unscathed.

I'm glad that both of my parents had no idea what terrible fate was awaiting them. Writing that you're going to be transported on the 9th. Murdered on the 12th. My sweet mother. I can't imagine it, and I try not to. It still keeps me awake at night sometimes. My father followed soon after. He was gassed on the 30th of April. Luckily it didn't take long before they were released from their suffering.

I couldn't stay with 'Uncle Co'. It was too dangerous. They didn't have any children and the neighbors might be asking themselves what this little boy was doing up there. Bear in mind that people in general couldn't be trusted any longer.

They took me with the VAMI cart to Curaçaostraat in Amsterdam where I ended up with a family of four: a father, a mother and their two children. It was a dreadful experience. Nobody talked to me and the children refused to play with me. During the day, after they had left for school, I was left to fend for myself, totally alone. In fact, it didn't really matter because when everybody was home I felt lonely as well without my parents, my Aunt Ju, my Uncle Louis and my own classmates. I was constantly being scolded as well, even though I had done nothing wrong. I hardly dared to move. I turned into a frightened little boy who rarely said a word. One particular event in Curaçaostraat, however, has remained etched into my mind forever.

One evening we were roughly awakened from our sleep. We shared one bedroom. The son and daughter slept in a nice big bed and I slept in a small child's cot. I was wearing the son's pyjamas because I didn't have any clothes of my own anymore. What was going on? They had apparently discovered a small turd in the hallway. Whose could it be? Nobody's? Not even Salo's? 'I guess we will have to inspect your bottoms,' said the 'aunt', who was called Jo. And so it came to pass. First the girl, Ansje: pyjama bottoms were lowered, buttocks spread followed by a wipe with a piece of toilet paper. There was nothing to report, the paper was clean.

Next in line was the son, Robbie. Again, the paper stayed nicely clean and white. Then it was my turn, the same ritual, only a bit more forceful. Pants down, legs spread, cheeks spread apart and a swift wipe. No, it couldn't be true. Yes, it was, there was brown on the paper and Aunt Jo shoved it right under my nose. Even though I really couldn't see anything, still, the culprit was Salo! I got a beating, a merciless beating, the first one in my young life and for the umpteenth time I cried myself to sleep that night.

The conclusion of the story was that I couldn't stay there any longer, not after such an 'incident'. After all, what kind of example would I be setting for the other kids! They decided that I had to move, this time to Amersfoort, with a family that had one son. A very nasty boy and so different from me. But... he owned a guitar! I thought that was great, except that I was not allowed to touch it. 'Not now or ever!' The lure of the guitar, however, won out over my fear of the boy.

I gathered my nerves and strummed a little tune. To my surprise, it sounded pretty good but my venture failed miserably. The boy barged into the room like a crazy person and started beating and kicking me. As I was lying on the floor with a terrible nosebleed he put the guitar back in the closet. I wasn't able to move, and my nose just kept bleeding. To my amazement, the boy's mother didn't punish him, she didn't even reprimand him. The only thing she said was: 'Salo, it was your own fault. You shouldn't have touched it and don't ever try doing it again!' Why I don't know, but as driven by a silent force, I did it again. Another beating followed. This time it was so bad that the doctor had to be called in. The diagnosis was serious bruises and a damaged nasal septum. 'He fell down the stairs, he was just careless,' they lied, with straight faces.

This time I decided not to let them get away with it and told the doctor what had happened, that the boy had beaten me up every time I had come near his guitar. I hadn't fallen down the stairs or been careless at all! It became clear that I couldn't stay there any longer either. But where was I to go next?

13 AN OLD, COLD BICYCLE

A man on a bike came to get me. It was an old, cold bicycle: I still remember it clearly. He lifted me onto the carrier and off we went to the train station. Great! I thought. We're going on a train. My very first time!

We got off in Koog aan de Zaan. Silently and very quickly we walked to our destination. When we arrived at a beautiful white house, surrounded by a green fence, the man opened the gate, walked up to the door and rang the bell. A woman opened the door. 'Is this the little boy?' she asked. Thus far, nobody had mentioned my real name. 'Salo' sounded too Jewish and thus too dangerous.

I was shown a small room, my own room, and new clothes. Finally, I was able to wear something different. The people were very friendly and the house was just beautiful. It had a huge yard. What else could I possibly wish for? The yard, especially, appealed to my imagination and to this very day it has remained the largest and most beautiful garden I have ever seen. I was permitted to play in it every day, except I was not allowed to shout, scream or laugh loudly, because no one was to know I was there. To play in front of the house was totally out of the question.

Uncle Bert was the director of a toy factory. His name was Van der Valk. Soon I felt so at home that I began to feel like myself again. I wasn't beaten, to the contrary they treated me with love and there was no 'bare bum inspection'! Mr. Van der Valk gave me a beautiful wooden rabbit, on wheels. I kept it with me throughout the war. Recently I gifted the rabbit to the Verzetsmuseum Junior in Amsterdam.

Still, there were questions that troubled me. Why didn't I hear anything from my father and mother? And what about the others? Wasn't anyone looking for me?

Life seemed to continue as normal, but not for the Jews. Fear began to take hold of them as reality began to catch up with imagination.

On August 7th, 1942 the Germans issued a new edict: the arrest of all Jews who refused to work in Germany. Deportation to Mauthausen followed, from where no one ever returned. The same would happen to Jews who refused to wear their Star of David or had changed their address without permission. Seyss-Inquart had launched this process of isolation as early as 1941. Jews had to report with the municipal or county registrar, where officials stamped a 'J' in their passport. Next, they had to fill out long lists of questions, which left nothing to conceal. Next, the mayors of the various cities forwarded the information to the Sicherheitsdienst, undoubtedly by order of the Germans, but still! It was the beginning of the end.

Was there no one who would try to help the Jews?

Some policemen in Amsterdam would give warning when yet another raid was being planned. The deportations occurred mainly with the aid of NSB agents and their cronies. The churches reacted only reluctantly, except on that one Sunday when a pastoral letter of protest was read ahead of the weekly sermon. They called on Seyss-Inquart to keep his earlier promise not to force anything onto our country that was foreign to us.

Some schools and universities protested against the despicable treatment of the Jews. The Dutch lawyer J.P.A. François remarked in his *Guidebook to International Law* that the laysoffs of Jewish civil servants, professors and teachers was not unlawful, given the pathological aversion held against the Jews by National Socialism, and which in turn stood in the way of any kind of cooperation with them. Jews just had to leave their workplaces and their professions willingly so as not to be gotten rid of in other ways.

The high-ranking Master of Law L.E. Visser, President of the Supreme Court, was 'discharged' without the slightest dispute. Students at the University of Delft protested the expulsion of several professors. It even ended up in a strike. Frans van Hasselt addressed the students during a meeting. It would turn out to be his final show of resistance. He died in the concentration camp of Buchenwald in 1942. In the city of Leiden non-Jewish professors and students protested, ending in the closure of both universities by the occupier. The Rector Magnificus of Amsterdam tried to prevent a strike and sent everybody on mandatory vacation. Eleven professors were ordered to be let go. In the cities of Utrecht, Groningen, Rotterdam and Wageningen, Jewish professors were kicked out. In total about 30 professors and teachers were forced to leave. The situation in the schools was the same, all Jews out. As a result many prominent scientists, professors and teachers disappeared forever. Many were angry and embittered that they had been met with so little compassion.

14 WHAT IS A JEW?

What had happened to the prewar respect and civility? Was it not of importance any longer? And what did they actually mean by 'Jews'?

'A Jew is someone who, according to race, descends from at least three full Jewish grandparents. Who has two full Jewish grandparents or who, on the 9th of May, 1940, had been a member of a synagogue or had become a member, shortly thereafter. Also he or she, who on that date or shortly thereafter, had married a Jew. A grandparent is considered fully Jewish when he or she was a member of a synagogue.'

The chief of the Amsterdam air-raid defense thought up the above. A variant is spelled out in an ordinance of January, 1941 when all Jews, including those who were half Jewish, and a quarter Jewish, had to register, because 'the Jewish influence on life in the Netherlands, as a whole, had become unbearable'. This directive would undoubtedly bring relief.

One had to register in writing. At that time there were about 100.000 Jews living in Amsterdam and every single one adhered to the order, because failure to do so was considered a crime. Registration involved the meticulous recording of personal data and these registration forms would seal the fate of the Dutch Jews. To make this directive a success it needed the cooperation of not only the Jews themselves but also the public servants. Orders were followed obediently. You could ask yourself why the Jews registered to begin with. Was it pride? Fear? The latter reigned without a doubt. After all where was one to go, or to turn, for help? Because of all sorts of measures, recommendations, publications and threats, the Jews became willing victims.

On September 5th the Germans had a complete overview: 160.820 registrations, 140.552 full Jewish, 14.549 half Jewish and 5.719 one quarter Jewish. Still, the agency involved was surprised by the low numbers. The Dutch authorities, however, had done their utmost to trace every Jew. On October 7th the job was completed, barely three months after the first deportation of Jews to unknown camps. With the use of the new lists Jews were dragged out of their homes by day and by night. Looking back, you could ask yourself: didn't the Jews see this coming? Something must have been known about the atrocities that were waiting them?

On November 8th, 1942 on the day the Allies landed in Morocco and Algiers, Hitler delivered a speech: 'If the Jews are thinking that they are capable of starting a world war with the purpose of destroying the European races, the result will not be the destruction of those races but the destruction of the European Jewry instead.

I was laughed at, but of those who laughed many don't laugh any longer, and those who are still laughing will, before long, not be doing that anymore.'

Looking back, it was clear language. But one could not possibly imagine what was facing the Jews, or was it that they didn't want to know? Fear pushed the reports about eradication into the background, but the reports became progressively larger in number. In June of 1942 the Russian radio announced the murder of almost all Jews who were living in the occupied territories of the Soviet Union.

One would think that due to the reception and interception of messages between Hitler's headquarters and the various German agencies, the English would have had knowledge of these mass murders. The BBC as well as Radio Orange didn't announce until June 26 / 27, 1942 that more than 700.000 Jews had been murdered in Poland.

There were other stories as well. Gerhard Riegner, the representative of the Jewish World Congress, charged that in the concentration camps experiments were taking place on Jews and subsequently their remains were turned into soap. Riegner, however, didn't attach too much value to those stories. He did believe another report, stating that 'by orders of Hitler, all European Jews should be destroyed by the fall of 1942 with the use of hydrocyanic acid'.

Riegner passed these reports on to the American and English consulates in Geneva, but there they stayed. They were simply not believed! In later broadcasts from Radio Orange the extermination camps weren't even mentioned. They were not mentioned by the Allies either: not a word about the gas chambers.

What were the governments to do? What to do with those millions of Jews? Large-scale help was impossible because that would give Hitler and his cronies a reason to move faster with his plan to exterminate all Jews. So, they kept silent.

As did Pope Pius XII. Many Jews converted to Catholicism, since that way they hoped to be able to count on the help of this pope. Forget it. Just once, during his Christmas message in December 1942, did he speak about the '100.000 people who, because of their nationality or race, were murdered'. It was said that the pope feared that an open protest would lead to an escalation of the persecution of the Jews and, I assume, the 25 million Catholics. Surely, he didn't want anything to happen to them. In short, Pius did not resist Hitler's crimes.

In a radio address to her citizens on October 17th, 1942, Queen

Wilhelmina expressed her repugnance for the systematic destruction of her Jewish citizens. But still, very few really believed what was going on.

15 ERADICATE ROOT AND BRANCH

The deportations were only talked or written about in hushed terms. What's more, no one even thought about 'extermination'. But let it be known that the anti-Semites didn't mind getting rid of the Jews. In June of 1942, a co-worker of *SS-Sturmbannführer* Willy Lages, by the name of Kempin, openly expressed 'that the Jews should be destroyed, root and branch'. Fischer didn't beat around the bush either when he said that 'it would be better if the Jews were destroyed'.

On March 22nd, 1943 Rauter gave a lecture in The Hague. In the presence of various officials in the SS, Rauter talked at length about prosecution of the Jews. Prof. L. de Jong included this lecture in its entirety in his historiography and I quote:

'It is known to everyone that there were about 140.000 'full' Jews in the Netherlands, including foreigners. Certain foreigners we were not able to arrest because of international reasons. However, the complete Jewry qualifies for deportation to the east.

I am able to announce within this circle (and I request you not to disclose this to the outside) that up till now we have already deported 55.000 Jews

47

to the east, and that 12.000 are still imprisoned. We hope that before long, not a single Jew will be left walking the street in freedom with the exception of mixed marriages with children and with them we still have a bone to pick. It's my goal to get rid of the Jews as soon as possible. This is not a pretty task, it's dirty work, but it's a measure that, historically, will be of great importance. We don't realize what it means to eradicate 120.000 Jews from a nation, who, a hundred years from now, could number one million. This measure of the German SS does stand for personal compassion, because the German people are backing us. The good we're doing for the people will take effect immediately and there is neither room for sympathy nor weakness. Those who do not understand this, or are filled with humanistic ideas, are not fit to lead. Especially a SS man has to forge ahead mercilessly and without compassion. All we want is to be cured of this disease. The Jewish problem has to be solved completely, once and for all.

During the past months, yes even in the past years, Adolf Hitler has addressed the problem over and over again. He has made it clear to the American Jewry and the Free Masons that, if the American capitalists would start a war and swoop down on Europe, it would mean the end of Jewry. That's the way it will happen. There will not be a Jew left in Europe...

I have decided that members of the police, who refuse to do their duty, will be thrown out.'

How the Jews would be destroyed, Rauter did not mention, at least not then.

I can't put it out of my mind that there was no one who knew exactly what was happening to the Jews. What about the escorts, who were supposed to keep order on the trains between Westerbork and Auschwitz and Westerbork and Sobibor? I will never know. Neither can I imagine how, on some of those trains, among all those innocent people, were my parents, my parents-in-law, my family and friends, trying to stand, sit or lie down. Did my parents still have the strength to think about me, their only son? That too, I will never know.

And what happened to those who collaborated with the Germans? Anyone who assisted in the arrests, the transportations and the plundering of homes was a collaborator. They too must have been aware of the fate of the Jews.

I don't want to go into all of the comments that were made about the Jews, but I do want to mention the one that was made by Rost van Tonningen: 'Just like before, I still consider every Jew as vermin... little by little we're making progress.' At the time he spoke those words, most Jews in the Netherlands had already been deported.

16 UNBELIEVABLE

Gradually the news about the fate of the Jews began to seep through. In early 1942, the German anti-fascist, Dr. Walter Bauer, told his friend, Dr. G.M. Borchardt, that all Jews in eastern Europe were being liquidated. It started out by shooting them or beating them to death. Later on they would be murdered by means of gas. He even discussed the technical details of the gassing procedures.

In May of 1942 two citizens of the Dutch province of Limburg returned from Auschwitz. One week prior to their release, the gassing in Auschwitz II (Birkenau) began on a large scale. The two men had to sign a declaration that they would never tell anyone what they had witnessed, but they did so anyway. Unfortunately, they were not believed. A twenty-two-year-old gardener took his story to the Jewish Council, but he was sent on his way!

And what about the story by J.H. Ubbink from the city of Doesburg, who had received extensive information from the German Kurt Gerstein, who in 1940 had infiltrated the SS? His sister-in-law had been gassed on the assertion that she was mentally handicapped. He inspected the disinfection installations of the Waffen-SS where Zyklon-B was used, similar to what was being used in the gas chambers. He had witnessed with his own eyes how in Belzec and Treblinka thousands of Jews were being gassed in this way. Gerstein and Ubbink reported all this information, but to no avail.

Dutch resistance newspapers, such as *Trouw*, *Het Parool* and *Vrij Nederland*, were apprehensive to print the stories. They reacted with total disbelief. However, in the September 27th, 1943 issue of *Het Parool*, a story appeared about the gas chambers, two days before the final, major roundup in Amsterdam. The well-known Amsterdam physician, I. van Hall, had become aware of these accounts. But even his colleagues in the Westerbork camp to whom he had told the stories had shrugged their shoulders. Maybe it was all about the power of imagination, for it was impossible to envision that one's parents, family, friends and many others had perished that way. People wouldn't do that sort of thing. Yet, they did!

The persecution of the Jews and the subsequent transports and extermination formed the most gripping events of the Second World War. They would also take the most victims.

On September 29th, 1943, 90.000 of the 140.000 full Jews had already been deported. Only a handful had been able to escape. About 11.000 were incarcerated in either Vught or Westerbork camps and 20.000 had gone into hiding, myself included. The occupier had at last succeeded, with the collaboration of many, through first isolating an entire part of the population to then move on to tear them away from society altogether.

Upon arrest, the Amsterdam Jews were taken to the Hollandsche Schouwburg and during the night they would be taken by streetcars to the train station. Across from the Hollandsche Schouwburg was a so-called daycare center, the same center where I was to spend a few days. Walter Süskind had been able to smuggle about a thousand babies to the outside. Sadly, Süskind himself was eventually caught. Many Jews were now trying to find hiding places, which demanded great courage from all parties.

17 DEATH PENALTY

Being caught, betrayed by neighbors or family or acquaintances, meant death for the person who had been hiding as well as the person who had offered his or her help. Nevertheless, about 20.000 people succeeded in finding a hiding place. But in the end, about half of them ended up falling into the hands of the Germans.

Many tried everything in their power to help the Jews, even some of the so-called 'good' members of the NSB. They would send out timely warnings when a roundup was anticipated and assisted in finding hiding places. This was for instance the case with the mayor of Winterswijk, NSB member Dr. W.P.C. Bos, who helped many citizens of his town to escape.

When, on the infamous September 29th, 1943, the last Jews were transported from Amsterdam to Westerbork to face their horrific deaths, many were still able to go into hiding. Most of them in their own country, others in Belgium and France and some even in Germany.

Betrayal was lurking around every corner at all times. Out in the countryside, where everyone knew each other, the risk of housing Jews had increased. It was especially the local members of the NSB, who liked to make a good impression, that were very dangerous. If they saw a chance to deliver Jews to the Germans in a merciless way, they not only handed over the Jews but the whole family they were hiding with as well. People trembled with fear. Fortunately some of the people living in the villages were extremely helpful to their Jewish fellow citizens. Just to mention a few, the nine Jewish citizens of Olst all survived the war. In Enkhuizen 52 out of 54 survived and in Tiel 67 out of 68.

In addition there were Jews who were not able to go into hiding. Either they had no place to stay or they lacked assistance. Not until after the war did it become clear that not enough helping hands had reached out. In contrast, it was much easier for non-Jews to find hiding places.

Then there was the question of when to go into hiding. Once a hiding place was located, that's when the dangerous work really started, such as getting hold of a new identification card. This meant that you were assigned a new name, a new address, a fake date of birth and sometimes you were suddenly either married or single. The people you were going to stay with had to know every bit of information and had to be able to memorize and recite it flawlessly. Now and then it occurred that someone's hair was dyed, preferably blonde, from the brown or black. Once all these details were taken care of you were ready to go into hiding.

It was a very emotional decision to have to leave your home and to say goodbye to family and friends, if they were still around. One wasn't allowed to take anything along. The Star was removed from one's clothing and then... gone, ready to be confronted with the unknown, to be handed over to strangers. Departure usually took place during the hours of darkness. Many were transported in crates, bookcases, on pushcarts, hidden between all kinds of stuff or between milk jugs. There were helpers, resistance workers, dressed in

German uniforms, which left you wondering sometimes if they could be trusted. Fear was deeply rooted.

Many Dutch people would have just about sacrificed anything to help the Jews, but the Germans, on their part, didn't leave a stone unturned to arrest them. Some non-Jews were being paid a high reward for betraying Jews. This reward varied from 7.50 to 37.50 guilders, which was a lot of money in those days.

People were also paid when they took someone in. Some time after the war a letter was found, stating that too little money was being received for taking me in. It turned out that the resistance was paying a weekly fee for me.

The (rather confusing) letter stated:

Drachten 9-9-'45

Dear Mrs.,

During his visit to family in Drachten, I heard the following:

They also visited Salo Muller in Amsterdam, who, as you know, is staying with his family in Biesboschstraat 50 on the second floor, in the south of Amsterdam.

There she heard that the family paid 44.60 guilders every month until August to a man named Piet (a pseudonym). But the family only received 12.50 a week. What happened to the rest? The family had also sent a package containing clothes and toys and a few new pairs of shoes. They received the toys, but the clothes and shoes never arrived.

There's a certain lady named Mrs. M (pseudonym) living in Leeuwarden who when I came looking for answers was very defensive and said: 'I will never give those clothes away.' And since this family also mentioned the name M I thought there might be some sort of a connection. The finances should be considered again, since these people are simple workers and they should still receive the money they were supposed to be paid.

The family thought Salo's family was well off and should easily be able to pay the overdue amount themselves.

Sincerely,

So my family, who had stayed in Amsterdam for a short while when I went into hiding, had paid money for me to do so.

It is very annoying that apparently Mr. P withheld the money. They corresponded about the money for years after. Letters were even sent to the court and also to Mr. P himself, a man who took in hundreds of children and thereby saved them. A man who was later even sentenced to death, but managed to get away. P was really upset about this.

'If money was withheld, this was spent on other children, weapons or food. It was never used for personal gain.' But still the correspondence never stopped. I even found a letter dated January 12th, 1960 from Leeuwarden. They still wanted to know to whom that money had been paid. The total amount was now about 2.500 guilders. They never found out what really happened. But with or without money, it was extraordinarily courageous of P and the others to save that many children.

Often it were the children who couldn't be kept quiet or a servant who had a slip of the tongue. Moreover, many homes weren't soundproof. There was no privacy and the little food that was available had to be shared. The question was: 'how long will this last'? It was hardly ever possible to go into hiding as a family, and contact with other members of one's family was forbidden. Many Jews had to pay for board. Everyone who was involved ran great risks, the Jews as well as the helpers. We must therefore have great respect for all the resistance workers who put their own lives in danger while trying to do everything possible to help their Jewish fellow citizens.

There were also Jews who, afraid to go into hiding themselves, would hand their children over to others, total strangers, which asked for courage beyond words. Just try to imagine having to give away your only child and sometimes all of your children to maybe never see them again. These were inconceivable decisions. My aunt and uncle made that decision for me. And I think my parents must have known somehow, since they sent that letter with the words: 'Say hello to Pietersen'.

18 AUNT JU AND COUSIN ETTY

One evening, an illegal worker came to Koog aan de Zaan to take me to the next address in Zaandijk. We left as soon as darkness set in. He did not hold my hand and at times I had to run to keep up with him. It was so dark outside. The night was so pitch-black, I could hardly recognize the man. The journey that followed was very long. A car and then another and after that a bike. It took very long and I felt extremely unsure of myself and afraid. Later I heard that the man took a detour on purpose, because he was scared of being followed.

Passing through a small backyard we ended up with the family Van Eijkeren. They immediately locked the backdoor and took me upstairs.

Guess who were there? Aunt Ju and cousin Etty! I still choke up when I think about it. Before I could utter a word, Mr. Van Eijkeren, whose name was Jaap, said: 'Remember, from now on Aunt Ju is to be called Aunt Suus, Etty is Paulientje, and their last names are Schut.' For a moment my head was spinning, then Aunt Ju picked me up and put me on her lap. Together we cried for a long time.

I must have sensed the seriousness of the situation because I never misspoke. The family Van Eijkeren was very kind to us. 'Uncle' Jaap was the principal of a Christian school. They were very religious people. They prayed before dinner and before they went to bed. I learned how to pray and how to say my prayers before I went to sleep. Needless to say, we were never allowed to swear, to talk loudly, to laugh or to sing. Not that we would do that very often anyway, but still.

Aunt Ju told me about Uncle Louis. He was hidden in Nederhorst den Berg and they called him Uncle Henk now. She could hardly control her emotions and did nothing but cry. She helped with the household chores, but due to her anxiety she dropped many cups and saucers. When that happened, Paulientje and I who would get an earful as well. Mrs. Van Eijkeren, boy could she rant and rave!

One evening the handicapped son of our neighbors came to visit. He was very tall with dark hair. He always wore a sleeveless pullover. He visited us quite frequently, much to Uncle Jaap's chagrin. The boy talked too much, as he was doing that evening.

Suddenly he said: 'I am going to tell everybody that Uncle Jaap is having people stay in his house.' The air became very heavy. We all looked at one another, but before we knew what was happening, Uncle Jaap began beating the boy. He went crazy. The stress that he had held back for so long was suddenly being released. He kept kicking the boy until he was lying like dead on the floor.

After some time when he slowly tried to get back up, Uncle Jaap pulled out a pistol and yelled: 'If you breathe one word about this to anybody, I will kill you,' after which the boy crawled, on his hands and feet, through the backyard back to his house.

As a result we had to leave immediately that same evening.

With the help of a very nice lady, Aunt Suus and Paulientje were able to move to Uncle Henk in Nederhorst den Berg. They moved in with separate families. My aunt and cousin were taken to a family working in a laundry called Portengen and Uncle Henk was staying with the family Hoetmer. Unfortunately, I was not allowed to join them, because that would have been way too dangerous.

Next, I was taken to Friesland by the well-known resistance worker, Piet Bosboom. Bosboom was a social worker who had been able to house many Jewish children, but eventually he was exposed by the Germans. When they came to arrest him, he got away by jumping out of a first-floor window, which caused serious injuries to his back and legs that would plague him for the rest of his life. For his courageous actions he received the Yad Vashem medal.

19 TREASON BY THE JEWISH COUNCIL

Due to the steady rumors and the desire for an end to the daily uncertainty, many Jews afraid to go into hiding went to the Jewish Council for protection. Dr. Presser called this organization 'a state within a state', a controlling body. The Jewish population hoped to receive either assistance or advice from the Jewish Council, if nothing else, but nothing could have been further from the truth.

The Jewish Council resided at Nieuwe Keizersgracht 58 in Amsterdam. In the first issue of *Het Joodsche Weekblad*, dated April 11th, 1941, the names of the members of the council were published: there were two chairmen, Messrs. J.R. Asscher and D. Cohen, as well as eighteen members, all men. One of these members was the powerful Max Bolle. Those who served on the council were exempt from deportation, at least for the moment. It was therefore of vital importance to be able to prove that one was working for the Jewish Council. Bolle compiled the lists.

The council had, of course, to comply with the Germans and their fanatical actions. Staff received a certificate that meant they were exempt from deportation since they were indispensable.

Jewish retailers and merchants were treated intolerably. Food was no longer available and the ritual slaughter of poultry was forbidden as well as the trade in fish.

The Jewish Council involved itself more and more with daily life, such as food aid and the supply of clothing. Various branches of the council kept themselves occupied with the 'common' people, Jews who found themselves in great need. They tried to get things done for themselves, their family and friends but didn't know to whom or where to turn. When someone tried to be placed on one of the lists for deferment or trade places with their parents, it would often come to blows. They were people fighting for their lives. Some tried to find employment with the Jewish Council, but most returned home empty-handed, left to their fate.

Because of the tremendous workload, which required more civil servants, the Jewish Council opened more offices but it was only allowed to congregate in front of the head office on Nieuwe Keizersgracht.

Dr. Edwin Sluzker, a lawyer from Vienna, became one of the most important members on the council. Most of the time he succeeded where Asscher and Cohen failed. Occasionally he was capable of dealing with Aus der Fünten. He knew the ropes and realized better than anyone how the German occupiers worked. He was also able to assist everyone who had problems with filling out the stacks of forms. When the deportations started, Sluzker tried to squeeze as many exemptions out of the Germans as possible. He also seemed to have had the strongest stomach for this dehumanizing work.

The worst department of the Jewish Council was located on Lijnbaansgracht 366, where the deportations of Jews were being prepared and the final lists were generated of who still needed to be deported to Westerbork and subsequently their death, but hadn't been caught yet.

In November of 1942, 600-800 people gathered daily at

Lijnbaansgracht, a number that would eventually grow to about 1.600 a day. At one of the other offices, at Afrikanerplein on Amsterdam's east side, 600 registered daily, at the office at Euterpestraat (now known as Gerrit van der Veenstraat) 250 and at the Lekstraat office about 60. At these locations heart-wrenching scenes could often be witnessed. The people who had gathered were told by the Jewish Council that they were to assist Jews who had been called up to go 'to work' in Germany as best as possible. However, the Jewish Council never advised anyone not to leave, to the contrary. It was understood that they had to go, and that they would never return.

The lists that were generated by the Germans described in detail what to bring on the trip. They had thought of everything, even books!

The Jews who arrived in Westerbork and needed 'further help' received assistance from the Jewish Council, department Oude Schans 74, where Mr. Blüth was in charge. The assistance went very well. Another department occupied itself with incoming mail but from the people who had been sent on not a single letter was ever received, not even from women and children. One was allowed to write from the Netherlands to family and friends who had already been deported. But these letters had to be written in German, so that the occupiers would be able to read them. Then these letters were translated by the Jewish Council. But more often than not the addressees had already met their death, gassed or killed in some other way. All Jewish Council collaborators received a (temporary) exemption from deportation so it goes without saying that many people wanted to work for them. People begged and fought to get on one of the deferment lists. When my Aunt Ju learned that her mother and grandmother had been called up, she went to pay Asscher, whom she knew, a visit to try and get them removed from the fatal list. It was in vain.

At the smaller departments of the council terrible things took place as well. In September, 1943 the department Home Care was eliminated. There were hardly enough Jews left, they were either deported, dead, had fled, or had been fortunate enough to have found a hiding place.

The Germans recorded everything meticulously and almost everyone participated with little or no protest. They demanded to find out everything that concerned the Jews, which was achieved through the Jewish Council. The council allowed itself to be used for everything. They met every request by the Germans, whose aim it was to create a defenseless and isolated segment within the nation. The council went along with it. No, it was actually worse than that, they never even put up any resistance or showed any solidarity with the people who were being deported. From start to finish, the Jewish Council insisted that the Jews should follow German orders and hiding was looked down at. They even offered assistance to those who were ready for deportation. The only opposition they offered was to delay and postpone, that was all. Presser wrote in his book *Extinction:* 'The Jewish Council allowed itself to be used to liquidate the complete Jewry in the Netherlands.'

Meanwhile parents tried everything possible to save their children from extermination. They handed them over to strangers. Some were even forced to marry employees of the council in order to save themselves. That way they would receive a 'sper', a stamp that would protect them as long as it suited the Germans.

In the end circa 25.000 Jews were fortunate enough to go into hiding with the help of loyal fellow countrymen. 3.000 were able to flee.

And what about the chairmen of this council, who were they and what did J.R. Asscher and D. Cohen do?

We understand that Asscher was a very Orthodox Jew and that the Germans were very pleased with him. This was one of the reasons why he was never replaced. Born on September 19th, 1880, Asscher was greatly respected during his lifetime and held important positions in the political world as well as the diamond business and in his own Jewish circles. Presser characterizes him as a naïve, impulsive and courageous man, who left the Jews in the lurch because he did not want to yield when it was still possible for them to leave. Some felt indebted to him. Others didn't and those that were deported and did not return can no longer speak. After the war he became afraid to face his fellow Jews, 'the remainder'. He died on May 2nd, 1950 and was buried in a non-Jewish cemetery.

The other chairman, Dr. David Cohen, was born on December 31st, 1881. He was a lot smarter than Asscher. But he too was guilty of helping the Germans eliminate the Jewish community. He was characterized by Presser as 'childish, domineering, opinionated and lacking character'. He, among others, did not want to admit that after the roundup of 1941 the Jewish Council had become an instrument for the Germans whose aim was to liquidate his fellow Jews. Cohen was the one who in 1942 encouraged the Jews to depart for the labor camps. Was there a difference between departure and deportation? He must have known because he did not give this advice to his family and friends. He was also in charge of the implementation of the wearing of the Jewish Star, which, according to the Germans, he carried out very well. No protesting, just do as you're told.

The Jewish Star had been issued in Germany on September 1st, 1941. All Jews, six years and older, had to wear, publicly, on the left side of their garment a yellow star where in the center, written in black, the word 'JEW' could be read. As of September 19th they were ordered to start wearing them. A bit later the Star had to be sewn on to other garments as well, such as work uniforms, shirts, and vests. In short, all visible clothing.

At the end of April, 1942 the Netherlands introduced the Star as well. Aus der Fünten told Asscher and Cohen that as of May 3rd every Jew had to wear a Star in public. Stars were even distributed to Jewish prisoners. There were all kinds of stipulations. The identification mark was a hexagonal star of yellow material (yellow is the color of humiliation), the size of the palm of your hand. The writing in the center imitated Hebrew. It had to be sewn on, not pinned or be attached in any other way. Difficulties quickly arose. Many felt very offended, but not obeying the order meant immediate arrest and being handed over to the Sicherheitspolizei, which undoubtedly meant certain death. To have to wear the Star created a sense of enormous humiliation and many Jews felt especially ashamed in front of their non-Jewish friends. The members of the Jewish Council were heavily criticized, however they cooperated fully to complete the operation within the set number of days. After all, it was important that the Jews would be able to buy their Star in time! It was also forbidden for Jews to wear any kind of medals or decorations. If they were caught doing it anyway, they would be sentenced to six months in jail and 1.000 guilders in fines. Unless, of course, they ended up facing a more serious punishment: death.

20   ORDERS FROM BERLIN

Assistance given to the Germans, especially by Cohen in regard to deportations, had among other things to do with the corrupt system of the so-called 'sperren' (deferment) through which one could give an unfair advantage to family, friends and acquaintances. How would the tens of thousands of gassed Jews have reacted to this? What would their attitude have been? Dr. Presser formulated his thoughts as follows:

'You were the tools of our archenemies. You have assisted with our deportations. This assistance was to save your own life. Your Council has lied, misled, harmed, humiliated and abused us. You continued to serve the mortal enemy, even when it had become unmistakably clear that all boys and men were being murdered. It was not us who appointed you as leaders, but our murderers and you didn't resign from your leadership. Worse, you forced us, using threats, to be slaughtered.'

I often wonder what my parents and my other family members would have said. It's incomprehensible to me that anyone could have deliberately executed these horrific orders, but Asscher and Cohen did exactly that.

And what happened to them after the war? The handful of Jews who returned broken and penniless complained to to the Department of Justice. Who had assisted? Asscher and Cohen. They came with rock-solid facts and factual complaints. In 1947 both men were arrested. A special council concluded that the order to create an 'Amsterdam Jewish Council' had been reprehensible as was the acceptance of the chairmanship, the continuation of the Jewish newspaper, after it had become clear that it benefitted the Germans more than it did the Jews, the assistance given to a number of anti-Jewish measures such as the giving out of the 'Jewish Star' and the mailings of directives when and how to depart for Westerbork and the assistance with the selection of deportation, especially in May of 1943, the time when my parents were arrested.

Based on these facts, the council advised to exclude Asscher and Cohen from honorary posts and paid functions of any kind with any Jewish agency, organization or institution for the rest of their lives. It was a clear case of solidarity with the Germans and it makes complete sense that Eichmann and Lages were very pleased with the work of the Jewish Councils.

Cohen passed away in 1967. Before he died he said that he continually asked himself how he could have done what he did.

But I am not yet finished with the Jewish Council.

Asscher and Cohen insisted repeatedly that the German rules were to be strictly followed, words that carried weight bearing in mind the trust that both men had enjoyed within the Jewish community. Looking back at February 20th, 1942 the relationship becomes quite clear.

That day, Asscher and Cohen called on all Jews in the Netherlands to follow German orders and stipulations and not try to back out of them in one form or another. 'You not only make it difficult for yourself, but possibly for the whole Jewish community!'

This was clearly blackmail of their own people. After all, they knew what fate was awaiting them. The council advised against hiding, and some people who could have gone into hiding didn't at the advice of Asscher and Cohen. Just like my own family. They did exactly what the Jewish Council told them to do. They never returned. Many of those that were caught hiding were taken away as special 'penal cases', not knowing what their fate would be. Or they did not want to know.

The organization of the council was excellent and effective. They had thought of everything. An order from Berlin would be flawlessly executed in the Netherlands, immediately if necessary. No one, however, would have thought that the war would last as long as it did. Had the war been over in 1942, Asscher and Cohen would probably have been thought of as heroes.

The local authorities and the municipal registries contributed greatly to the registration of Jews and the stamping of the distinct 'J' inside the ID cards. A valuable collaborator turned out to be I.B.M. Hollerith, son of a German immigrant, Herman Hollerith, who landed a job with the American Census Bureau upon receiving his engineering degree. The operations at the American Census Bureau were very complicated and time-consuming so Hollerith designed a machine that was capable of storing hundreds of pieces of information on punch cards, and could not only quickly process them but also sort, alphabetize and select them. The machine became a huge success and IBM leased it all across the globe.

In the thirties IBM had business dealings with Germany, with Hitler to be precise, and IBM's German sister company was soon able to register every Jewish citizen in all of Europe in an easy way. The horrendous transports to the concentration camps and the gassings were also organized through the Hollerith machines. In a book that was published not too long ago, titled *IBM and the Holocaust*, the author Edward Black, son of Polish Jewish parents, explains the situation down to the smallest detail. The number tattooed on my parents' arms and their cause of death – 'B-gassing' – were also indicated on these punch cards, as 'number F6'.

Through the diligence of the civil servants who worked for the Dutch registry, the Netherlands became the leader in the number of murdered Jews. After the war it turned out that almost 75% of the Jewish population had been murdered. I would also like to mention that all of the civil servants had signed the 'Non-Jew Declaration' and thus had a hand in the firing of Jewish civil servants working at employment offices, on streetcars, the railroads and on the police force. They assisted willingly with arrests and deportations. With the exception of a few, no streetcar- or train conductor was known to have performed these sinister tasks, but the police? They made sure that everything went off without a hitch.

The guards in Westerbork stood out in the sense that they worked under the control of the Dutch military police. Dutch government agencies participated in the seizure of radios, bicycles and the disconnection of telephone services. The banks also did their share and promptly transferred the Jewish account balances to Lippmann Rosenthal. The stock market did not allow the sale of Jewish stocks. Even the permits of Jewish stockbrokers were recalled.

Asscher and Cohn were not in the least troubled by these measures. They were allowed to keep their telephones, their radios and their bicycles. They were allowed to ride the trains, the streetcars and even in their automobiles – 'to perform their duties'.

In May of 1943 the Jewish Council had to identify 7.000 for deportation. A dreadful task, but still they compiled this hit list. Many of my relatives were on this list. Begging and praying they tried to trade places or get a deferment. In vain!

My Aunt Ju fought with her mother to be allowed to trade places with her. She begged on account of her grandmother, 'Please leave these kind people at home! Let me go instead!' Asscher and Cohen threw her out of the office. She did not know then that her mother and grandmother had already died in Auschwitz.

In spite of all of the Germans' promises, in the end Asscher and Cohen were sent to Westerbork. Dr. Presser writes: 'Cohen was deliriously happy when he finally took a seat on the train to Westerbork. It had bothered him greatly to watch the trains leave.'

Asscher and Cohen had to take on their duty as chairmen of the Jewish Council once more. It was on September 19th, 1943, when Aus der Fünten told them that the council had been disbanded.

21 A GREAT LOVE: GERMANY

Who were those people in the Netherlands the Jews were so fearful of, and who were at the beck and call of the Jewish Council?

First of all there was Seyss-Inquart, born on July 22ⁿᵈ, 1892 in Maravia, the youngest of six children: their father, Catholic, and their mother, Lutheran, subjected their children to a very strict upbringing. Seyss-Inquart successfully finished high school and went on to study law in Vienna. He paid his way through university by tutoring Jewish children!

According to himself, however, he loathed the Viennese 'Jewish clique'. His great love was Germany. During the First World War he fought on the Italian front, for which he received a distinguished service medal for bravery and was promoted to Oberleutnant. In 1916 he married Gertrud Mischka, the daughter of an Austrian general. They had three children.

As early as 1919 Seyss-Inquart became a member of an anti-Semitic organization, a 'Society of Gentlemen' in Vienna. He didn't have any real friends, but one great passion: classical music. In Austria he became the Germans' highest representative. He was easily recognized from his limp due to a crushed kneecap. He adored Hitler and was of the wistful opinion that Germany would win the war. On May 10th, 1940 Hitler sent him to the Netherlands in the post of Reichskommissar, although he didn't speak a word of Dutch.

Next, there was Hanns Albin Rauter, also born in 1892, in Klagenfurt, Austria. He was one of seven siblings. He was well known as an officer in the Austrian-Hungarian army, and he too was promoted to Oberleutnant. During the war Rauter became the symbol of Nazi terror in the Netherlands. In contrast to Seyss-Inquart, the Jews feared him immensely.

Third in line was Willy Lages. Under the command of Himmler, the notorious, most cunning and most cruel leader of the Sicherheitsdienst, he occupied an important post with the police in the occupied Netherlands.

In February of 1941 he settled in the capital with the assignment to track down the instigators of the February Strike. He stayed in the service of the 'Central Government' and, with the cooperation of Ferdinand aus der Fünten, he executed orders received from Germany to do with the destruction of the Jews.

As these gentlemen went about their pernicious tasks, assisted by many countrymen, while others watched passively, thousands, who were in danger, had to try and find a safe hiding place.

Like myself.

22 JAPJE IN FRIESLAND

Piet Bosboom took me to my new hiding place. This time I went to Friesland, Drachtstercompagnie. I remember it as being a long and tiring trip. Finally we reached the tiny village of Ureterp. The place we were supposed to go to was a small farm, situated a little way off the muddy main road with lots of puddles. When we reached the farm I noticed chickens, a dog and a cat wandering around the yard.

Everyone shook hands when we walked into the house: there was a father, a mother and a son. The mother's name was Ansje, the father was called Anne and the eldest son, Rein. Besides Rein they had yet another son and two daughters.

They were very nice people, but I had a difficult time understanding them because they spoke Frisian. Besides being a farmer, Anne also transported milk. Early in the morning he would go out with his horse and wagon to pick up the full milk cans that other farmers had put alongside the road to take them to the town of Drachten. Later in the day, he would return the empty cans and put them back alongside the road near the farm where he had picked them up. Anne often took me along. Sometimes I was even allowed to steer the horse. That was really exciting. I would be calling out the commands loud and clear to make sure the horse would listen to me, or so I thought. Later I came to understand that the horse had made the trip back and forth to Drachten so often that it would have found its way home without anyone driving the wagon.

I played with Rein frequently and every so often with his sister, Neeltje. But we also had to lend a hand outside. At first I found it very difficult, due to my lack of understanding of the language, but since there wasn't anything else spoken, I soon became quite fluent in Frisian.

I also met other family members, aunts, omkes (uncles) and Pake and Beppe (grandfather and grandmother). I was introduced to them as cousin Japje from Limburg. Limburg is one of the southern provinces whose population in general has dark features. I was said to be the son of Beppe's younger sister. My name was changed from Jaap to Japje. Jaap was for older people, while I was still very young as well as very short and skinny for my age. I adjusted quite rapidly because I knew I had to. But still there were a lot of things that seemed foreign to me.

For instance, I had to walk in wooden shoes. I owned two pairs, one for during the week and the other for church. Every Sunday I would go to Drachtstercompagnie, first to the church and afterwards to Sunday school.

Just like all the other kids I had to learn to recite a psalm. When the pastor was satisfied he would give me a sticker to put in a booklet. I earned a lot of stickers! I was still the quiet, nice little boy, who had to obey everybody. And of course there were always questions such as: 'Where are you from?', 'Where are your parents?', 'When is your birthday?' Actually, I didn't know anything. I couldn't answer a single question and that seemed a bit fishy at times.

Often we could hear planes fly over and occasionally there were bombings. When the English were bombing a neighboring German camp, it meant that we immediately had to lie down on the floor. The

74

neighbouring camp was the infamous Trimunt. In the fall of 1940 a German radar station was set up near Trimunt in Friesland. The Germans also built barracks for hundreds of German soldiers. The barracks were built on a piece of land that was owned by a farmer called Wiegersma, who later took me in. The information that was gathered at Stelling Trimunt allowed the Germans to take down many Allied planes.

In 1944 the Germans were afraid of air raids on the radar station. They decided to build some bunkers for the safety of the soldiers. The bunkers (or the ruins) can still be visited today. They are close to highway A7. A motor race course was also built next to those bunkers.

23 LIFE AND DEATH EVERY DAY

Anne wanted to see me one evening. He told me that some people had found out that I was a Jewish boy, which meant that I could no longer stay on the farm. I would be taken somewhere else. They knew who had betrayed me and they would be paying for it.

They took me to the grocer Van Dijk, who had a small barn behind his store. Accompanied by two bigger boys, I stepped inside. There was hay all over the place. Rein, who had come along, told me that the boy who was working here had betrayed me.

Moments later the grocer and his son walked into the barn. I shook their hands. 'Japje, why don't you go and stand over by the door and don't look!' Still, I took a peek! I watched a boy enter the barn with a wheelbarrow filled with hay. The grocer's son had grabbed a pitchfork and walked toward him. 'Klaas, do you know what we do to traitors around here?' Before I realized what had happened, the farmhand was on the floor, screaming as I watched the grocer's son stab the boy a few times in the stomach. Suddenly the screaming stopped. The boy didn't move and there was a puddle of blood on the floor. I almost threw up.

'He will not betray anyone anymore!' Van Dijk said.

I wasn't able to sleep for quite a long time. I couldn't talk to anyone about it, but I guess it was alright to pray, so I decided to tell myself about it or could it have been Jesus after all? I also answered myself, that way I knew exactly what I had to do.

A couple of days after the event with the pitchfork, a quiet Sunday morning, we didn't go to church as usual. Instead I was told to dress casually, no Sunday wooden shoes and no cap. Anne drove the horse and wagon into the yard and asked me to sit next to him. He was going to take me to the son of Omke, Beppe's husband. That's how I ended up in Ureterp, this time on a real farm.

24 AMONG MICE AND RATS

The next family, Mr. and Mrs. Wiegersma, had two sons. Besides me there were two other boys, who were living in the attic. They were from Rotterdam. I rarely saw them and I didn't ask any questions about them. I was living in a suspended world.

However, I thought about my parents a lot and I just didn't understand why I hadn't seen or heard from them. I also missed Aunt Ju and Uncle Louis.

I was eight now and joined the family in their work in the field. It was pretty hard work, I must say, but Mr. and Mrs. Wiegersma were wonderful to me. They treated me as one of their own. It was always very busy on the farm, because of a German camp that had been set up nearby. The Germans came to get butter, cheese, eggs, milk and other supplies every day, which meant that there was not much left for us. Occasionally I still felt hungry after dinner and we were allowed to put cheese rinds on top of the potbelly stove, so that we could eat them burnt and warm. A real feast!

At times, when the farmer didn't have or didn't want to give the

Germans the supplies they wanted, he was beaten by the soldiers. Slowly, I must have become aware of what was going on.

I shared a box-bed with the two sons while the Rotterdam boys slept in the hayloft. Because I cried a lot, they let me search for lapwing eggs all by myself, even though it was not yet the season for them. The real reason for sending me away was that the people who were coming to visit the farm were not allowed to see me. It was all related to some cute young girls, that much I had been able to figure out. In the evenings, there would sometimes be six of them at a time. I didn't know them. They always sat in the front room of the house.

One day the farmer was hauled away in an open military vehicle. He had been quarreling with some of the German soldiers. Apparently, he had refused to do 'something'. There was a lot of yelling back and forth. When he returned home that evening, he had a swollen face, black eyes and there was blood everywhere. From that day on I was no longer allowed to sleep in the box-bed.

After dark, one of the boys would come in and lift a few floorboards, using a pair of pliers. When they figured the hole was big enough, they would grab me by my hands and lower me into it. Once I was seated on the floor below they would rearrange the boards. It was awfully cold down there and there were mice and rats everywhere, but still I was not allowed to make any noise, no matter what, because if the soldiers would find me they would kill me.

Here it was where I learned the true meaning of the word fear.

Often they had me helping with the harvesting of the potatoes. Among the potatoes there were hundreds of mice. They were afraid of nothing and just climbed onto your legs. I hated it. I still really dislike mice!

It was Sunday once again. Standing in front of the window I seemed to notice Omke in the distance. He was seated in some sort of Jeep. He was wearing his usual blue-black shirt and his cap. I called out that Omke was coming.

That's when everything completely changed. Amid a lot of screaming and yelling, the two people from Rotterdam were sent away. They jumped down from the hayloft and ran towards the ditch. Then the sound of gunshots followed.

Behind the farm German soldiers were running to and fro. The men from Rotterdam had run into the water and swum into the reeds. I never saw them again.

In the meantime the farmer was yelling at everybody. He opened the window, firmly seized me and put me outside, calling: 'Japje, run as fast as you can, go and look for lapwing eggs and wait until somebody comes to get you!'

So it hadn't been Omke, who I had seen coming down the road. It had been an organized raid.

I walked for hours through the fields and, of course, didn't find a single egg. I became tired and very scared. I saw German soldiers strutting around everywhere. Against all warnings, 'Whatever happens, never go near that camp!', I began to do just that. Fortunately no one detected me or wanted to detect me, so I lay down in the grass and began talking to myself again. Eventually, Aunt Anna came to get me. 'Am I allowed to go back home now?' I asked. Sadly that was no longer possible. The Germans had arrested the farmer and there were all kinds of strange people walking around on the farm.

'You're going to Beppe and Omke,' she replied.

25 WIPING MY BEHIND WITH A SHEET OUT OF THE PSALMS

So it was that when darkness had set in, I was picked up by a stranger. I had to go with him seated on the carrier of his bike. He didn't speak a word. I was very cold and very scared. After some time we passed Anne's farm. We had to go a little further yet. Beppe and Omke were living in a small house, a farm of some sort. It was very cold and dark. When I entered the living room, I noticed a little boy. 'His name is Sjors,' Beppe said, 'you may shake hands with him.' Sjors was another Jewish boy that Beppe had taken in. His name was actually Sal and he was also from Amsterdam.

But the little boy didn't want to. Here, too, was a box-bed, in which I had to sleep together with Sjors. There was no light, no toilet, no water, actually there was nothing. Outside there was a 'huuske', which served as a toilet and to wipe our behinds we used a piece of paper, most often a page out of the Psalms from a calendar. We got water from the drainpipes.

During the day, when people were passing by, I had to go and sit in the chicken coop. 'No talking and absolutely no yelling.' I would just lie down on the straw or sit somewhere. I was not allowed to move at all, because the chickens might get scared and start moving around.

Beppe was just wonderful. She had beautiful, long gray hair, which she brushed every morning after which she rolled it up and twisted it into a bun. I watched her do it every morning in total silence. I thought Beppe was beautiful! At times I thought she looked like my grandma. Did I actually have a grandma? Did I actually have a father and a mother? How old was I really? The older I got, the more often these questions seemed to occupy my mind. Why did everybody leave me?

I became ill, began to stutter, started to cough and picked up an itch all over. The doctor came on his motorbike. 'That little boy is very ill,' he said. It turned out that I had become asthmatic due to the moisture and the mold on the walls. I had also become allergic and eczema and lice had begun to cover my whole body. The doctor prescribed a cough medicine and furthermore I had to be washed twice a day with paraffin oil. Every day they combed my hair with a special comb. I allowed it all without complaining. What else was I to do?

Omke was a quiet, small man. He chewed tobacco and sometimes he would walk outside to spit it out. When it was really cold, he would take the lid of the heater and spit into the fire. Beppe was always mad at him for doing this, but he didn't care one bit. I kind of liked it, but I was not supposed to laugh about it!

Sometimes Anne and Omke slaughtered an animal in the small shed. At times they let me watch, but I was a little scared.

Sjors and I didn't really get along. He was a nasty boy, who always wanted to fight. And on top of that he lied. He blamed me for everything.

Often Beppe became angry and fell on the floor in convulsions. She was suffering from epilepsy. It was awful to watch and we were not allowed to touch her. Omke always said that it would go away by itself, but it could take quite a while before Beppe would 'wake up' again. I couldn't stand the smoke that was coming out of the heater.

But when Beppe could stand up again, she would sit by the heater and stoke the fire even more.

Once a week I had to churn milk to make butter. I had been taught how to milk while I was staying with Anne and that came in handy. I often went for a walk in the pasture and when I became thirsty, I would take a cup and walk up to one of the cows and fill my cup with wonderful, warm milk. Very rarely did I play with other kids. When I did, it was mostly with Rein and Neeltje. They lived close to us. However, I was not allowed to tell them who I was and where I came from. That was not too difficult, since I didn't know myself!

I had an easy life, because I was often sick, which didn't allow me to do much.

Here too, English airplanes often flew in the direction of the German camp. We always went to bed early because there was nothing to do during the evening. There were no books to read. But could I even read? Did I forget how to, or did I never learn? I don't know anymore. Neither did we have a radio. There was nothing, only a kerosene lamp in the middle of the room.

My days were very long. I had little to do. In the morning I got up early. We ate a homemade sandwich with jam or cheese. In the afternoon we had a hot meal. We would get a plate and in the middle of the table there was a pan with potatoes and a separate pan with gravy. You could serve yourself. Sometimes we ate porridge instead.

At night we would eat a sandwich again with homemade rye bread with bacon that we smoked ourselves. We also drank milk, mostly straight from the cow.

During the day, Sjors and I played inside. Mostly separately. I don't remember exactly what I played with. I didn't have anything. I just had my wooden rabbit, but I didn't play with it anymore.

A good part of the day I spent in the chicken coop, away from Sjors.

Very few people ever visited. In any case, I was not allowed to talk to them – only if Beppe or Omke told me so.

I had a good relationship with the family doctor. At times he told me things about the war and about what the resistance members did. But he also told me that there were camps, where almost all the people were being killed. 'Yes, Japje, also in Holland.'

26 DUTCH CONCENTRATION CAMPS

Where were these Dutch concentration camps? In 1943 there were 8.500 prisoners in the Amersfoort camp, among them about 1.000 Jews. Of these, 800 were deported to Mauthausen while 200 were sent on to Westerbork. Life in the Amersfoort camp was very difficult, especially because of the camp commandant J.J. Kotälla, a true executioner. The Jews, especially, suffered enormously. Life in the Ommen camp was also a living hell. From here, many prisoners were sent on to Westerbork.

Camp Vught sounded like a curse. It consisted of 36 living / sleeping barracks and 23 work barracks. It was surrounded by a very high barbed-wire fence and behind it a canal with sloping barbed wire, and then yet another high barbed-wire fence. At every 50 meters there was a watchtower, manned by a member of the SS, with a searchlight and a machine gun. The camp was financed with money stolen from Jews, and built by the Dutch.

The camp commandant, Karl Walter Chmielewski, born in Frankfurt in 1903, had been the camp leader in the notorious Mauthausen between 1940 and 1942. He was a known alcoholic, a womanizer and a loafer. He was in charge of the SS at the camp, who had come out of the underbelly of society: thieves, murderers, gamblers, and so forth. The kapos consisted mainly of Germans and Poles from other camps. They undoubtedly must have known about the gassings. Camp Vught was a transit camp for Jews. When they arrived here from the Hollandsche Schouwburg in Amsterdam or the camp in Amersfoort they were humiliated, beaten or mistreated in some other way. In September of 1943 the camp counted 12.000 prisoners: 10.000 were sent to Westerbork, while 2.000 were eliminated. In June of 1944 the camp was cleared out and closed.

The deportation of Jews in our country began in February of 1941 and lasted until September of 1944. Most of the Jews were housed in Westerbork in the province of Drenthe before being deported to various extermination camps. The first deportation train left in July of 1942. Among those being deported for extermination were my parents and the rest of my family. 51 of these deportations to Auschwitz took place on a regular basis, usually two trainloads per week. People had become terrified of these deportations. They asked themselves: 'Will I be leaving by myself or are my husband or wife and children able to come with me?' It was a fear that drove people crazy. Each time about 1.000 Jews left for the camp!

The security of the camp was entrusted to the Dutch police. Registration took place on arrival and was carried out by Jewish camp personnel following which prisoners were sent to the camp, meaning barracks, mud, sand, watchtowers and barbed wire. The camp had been built before the war on the authority of the government. It was intended as an arrival camp for Jewish fugitives from Germany. Outside the camp Dutch police stood guard.

In the meantime the camp commandant SS Obersturmführer Gemmeker made camp inmates work 60 hours per week. Not only was life horrific but the fear of the inmates must have been beyond words. Among them were my parents and family members. Were they thinking of me? What must have gone through their minds? Just imagine losing your only child, to have been forced to leave your only child behind. I still struggle, almost daily, with these thoughts. On the other hand, maybe they were happy that I had been spared this horror.

In my mind I see them sitting in Westerbork, early on in the war in 1942. They stayed there for ten weeks. Along with thousands of others they were deported in cattle cars to Auschwitz, just because they were Jewish. And the questions keep coming: was there nobody who could do something? Was there nobody who could have sabotaged the trains or blown up the tracks? How come they were not able to flee? Impossible! Every morning an extremely thorough roll call took place and if an inmate came up missing, ten other inmates were punished by being deported instead.

27 A TRAIN FROM APELDOORN

On the 22th of January in 1943 a train arrived from Apeldoorn, a special transport with people who were mentally ill. Among them were two of my aunts, my father's sisters. They were suffering from hormonal imbalance, for which there was no cure in those days. They were sent to Apeldoorn because they were acting a little 'strange'.

On December 31st, 1942 the Jewish mental health clinic in the Apeldoorn forest counted 1.100 patients, women as well as men, and a staff of 500. The connected clinic Paedagogium Achisomog counted 94 children. No one could have imagined the kind of tragedy that would soon take place here. People knew that the Nazis not only wanted to eradicate the Jews, but the mentally ill as well. On November 6th, 1942 the director, Dr. Loostein, had already been informed that the Germans wanted to close 'Het Bosch', as it was called. The reason given was that they needed the building for themselves. The director didn't take any action, largely because he couldn't and wouldn't believe that the Germans were capable of doing such a thing. He never thought that they would deport the mentally ill. They couldn't possibly be that bad?

Then came an order from Eichmann in Berlin: he wanted 'Het Bosch' vacated, and a train consisting of 25 cars would soon follow. On January 19th information was received from the police commissioner that the whole place had to be made Jew-free and on January 20th 100 men, responsible for keeping order in Westerbork, arrived and demanded accommodation. A number of nurses panicked and 100 fled that same night. What to do with the patients, the mentally ill, the deranged, the demented, the schizophrenics, the feeble-minded and the psychopaths? They didn't have to wait long for an answer, because on the night of January 21st Aus der Fünten himself came to visit. Dr. Presser conveyed the incident as follows: 'That night there was a lot of cursing, gross maltreatment and stealing going on. Besides the patients, they also took a number of 'normal' Jews with them, who happened to live in Apeldoorn. Adults and children, people who had been hiding in the clinic where they thought they would be safe.'

The transport must have been merciless. First in trucks, and from there in waiting trains. Of the accompanying nursing personnel, who had been assured by Aus der Fünten that they would be allowed to return, no one survived. On arrival in Auschwitz all patients were gassed immediately.

Orphans and foster parents met with the same fate. On April 14th, 1943 the Germans sent out notifications that the children would be picked up together with their foster parents. They would go to Westerbork first, only to meet their fate from there. In case a lone parent had been picked up, the Germans would show their 'compassion' and wait until the other parent had been picked up as well. After all they wanted to keep families together.

From Westerbork 34.000 Jews were deported to Sobibor. Only 19 survived that living hell. My wife's parents were not among them. Another 60.000 Jews were deported to Auschwitz-Birkenau. Those transports must have been heart-wrenching, with people leaning against each other and lying on top of one another in jam-packed cars.

Excrement and urine were flowing freely, since there were no toilets, apart from maybe a small barrel. Occasionally the train would stop briefly and German attendants would enter the cars to rob the prisoners of anything of value that they might still be carrying on them: watches, rings, gold and money. Those transports lasted about 80 hours. Many did not survive, they died of suffocation. The Germans, who escorted the transport, usually about 15 of them, would be riding royally in a coach.

I often imagine my wonderful parents in one of those wagons on their way to meet their deaths. They would not be counted among the 500 virtual skeletons that were liberated at the end of the war.

It is difficult to imagine, in the time in which we are living now, that we believed the following garbage. The *Hamburger Fremdenblatt* of July 24th, 1942 printed the following article: 'We received news from Amsterdam that the Dutch citizens are treating their Jewish fellow citizens in a heartless manner. As a result the Jews have asked the Wehrmacht for protection. In spite of the centuries-old hostility, the German army has taken the Jews into their protection and, at the Jews' own request, has transported them to Germany, where they will be allowed to carry out their professions in peace and quiet. Out of gratitude the Jews have handed their furnishings and jewelry over to the homeless in Germany, whose homes had been ravaged by English bombers.'

Meanwhile, however, the trains continued moving along and the Germans were happy. If things would continue this way, and they would, the 'Jewish problem' would soon be solved. The Dutch police took the Jews in and held supervision. The Jewish Council, on the other hand, took care of the arrests, the support system and maintaining an orderly course of action. Others, non-Jews, also pulled their weight. *De Telegraaf* noted on June 15th 'that the Nazis would relentlessly pursue the total destruction of the Jewry'.

It is unbelievable that no one came to any independent conclusion, but kept following orders without giving them any thought.

On August 2nd, 1942, Schmidt spoke on behalf of the occupied forces. He noted that 'The Jew was Germany's worst enemy. Jews had to leave the west. They had to go to the east to work and to make up for everything they had done. But... we are no barbarians, we want the Jews to be joined with their families. However, they will have to start rebuilding the devastated east. Their fate will be gruelling, but don't forget, they entered our country as poor as church mice.'

Finally, the Jews began to realize what was going on, which resulted in a drop in the number of voluntary applications. As a matter of fact there weren't enough to make up a transport. The Jewish Council had to come to the rescue!

28 BLACK THURSDAY

Meanwhile, the Germans had planned a huge roundup in Amsterdam for Thursday, August 6th, 1942, which would go down in history as 'Black Thursday'. The goal was to capture 2.000 Jews.

From dawn till dusk Jews were stopped in the streets or dragged out of their homes. Resisting the Grüne Polizei and the black-shirted members of the NSB was nearly impossible. Those that were arrested were immediately taken to Adema van Scheltema Square. 600 left immediately for Westerbork and from there were moved on to extermination camps.

Sadly, there was no one who properly advised the Jews, not even within their own circle. To the contrary. A special edition of the Jewish newspaper, dated August 7th, 1942 stated the following:

1. Jews who do not comply immediately when summoned for labor expansion in Germany will be arrested and deported to Mauthausen. This punishment does not apply to Jews who will still be registering on August 9th, 1942 but no later than 5:00 p.m., or those who state that they are willing to participate in the labor expansion.

2. Jews who are caught not wearing the 'Jewish Star' will be deported to Mauthausen.
3. Jews who change their place of residence or home, even for a brief period, without approval of the authorities, will be deported to Mauthausen.

It was quite clear that statements 2 and 3 pertained to those Jews who had gone into hiding and those who were still trying to get away.

The Jewish Council sent employees on home visits to encourage people to comply. Still, in spite of the grave punishments that were waiting in store for them, many Jews fled to the south via Belgium.

But the roundups did not end there. They would continue until the last Jew had disappeared from the public scene. Initially, the Jewish Council had prepared a list of Jews who were 'indispensable', but before long the Germans began to whittle down that list as well.

By October 24th, 1942 about 20.000 Jews had been deported in our country alone. The Germans tried to deport another 30.000 before Christmas of that year. On October 15th Rauter declared Jews to be 'outlaws'. Even the old, the sick and the defenseless Jews in rest homes and hospitals didn't receive deferment.

29 NAKED IN THE COLD NIGHT: TOWARDS MEETING THE END

On arrival in Auschwitz people were robbed of all their possessions by Jews who belonged to the Kommando, through promises that everything would be returned later. Those Jews who were to be gassed immediately were led away. Those who were still able to work were spared temporarily. Men and women were separated. The elderly and mothers with children had to stand in line. The remaining men and women were split into two rows.

That's the way they dealt with my parents, some of the first to enter Auschwitz, via the former theatre in Amsterdam and Westerbork.

From July 15th, 1942 until February 23rd, 1943, 52 transports arrived in Auschwitz. My parents were on the first one. Of the first transport of 42.945 people, only 12.001 were registered as prisoners, the remaining 30.944 were gassed immediately.

The Jews were gassed in two bunkers that looked like farmhouses with thatched roofs. After you were taken there by truck, you were told to take a shower in either Bunker 1 or Bunker 2 for for sterilization purposes. While still in their barracks they were told to undress, men and women separately. From there they were to walk in completely naked to meet their fate.

This is what happened to my parents.

How were they and their relatives murdered? This is what I dream about, this is why I'm often troubled. It keeps me busy day and night and there is always that question: 'How was this possible? And why did it happen?'

Once the defenseless, scared, tired and hungry people were inside, the doors were immediately bolted. Then arrived the barrels of Zyklon-B, the pulverized shells of shellfish saturated with liquid cyanide. At a temperature of 18° Celsius this highly poisonous matter turns into a gas. That's why the barracks were sufficiently warmed up ahead of time. The result was inescapable death. People suffocated under the most horrible circumstances. Wearing gasmasks, the members of the SS scattered the Zyklon-B through holes in the sidewalls into the gas chambers and the incredible agony lasted a few long minutes.

When, after some time, the gas chamber became ghostly quiet, the SS guards would peek through the holes to makes sure everybody was dead. At that point they allowed the cyanide gas to escape and a Sonderkommando of Jewish prisoners was called inside. They carried the dead bodies out on sheets. Professor De Jong explains it in detail: 'They were still warm, wet from sweat, often covered with urine, excrement and vomit.'

The women's hair was cut off and mouths were checked for gold or platinum fillings and crowns.

Until September, 1942 the prisoners were still digging graves in which they dumped the bodies of those who had been gassed. And this is where my parents, my grandfather and grandmother, uncles, aunts and cousins are as well, among thousands of nameless Jews. No grave that I could occasionally visit with a bouquet of flowers or to talk to them and to tell them what happened to me, their only son. But maybe they are able to see everything from beyond.

Later on, the bodies were burned outside on large grilles. Then they dumped the ashes in the marshes close by. From 1943 onwards the bones of these bodies were sold to a German corporation! Everyone from the Sonderkommando in the camp knew that if they resisted in any way, immediate death would follow. If someone from the Sonderkommando would tell what fate the prisoners were awaiting in the showers, he would be burned alive on the grilles besides the bodies of those who had been gassed.

My parents were not killed immediately. They were young, healthy individuals. My mother was a very pretty woman with long black hair. My father was tall and slender. I have one picture left, which was taken at the seaside resort of Scheveningen, on the beach. I'm sitting on my father's knee and my mother is smiling broadly.

The last months of their lives they lived separately in Auschwitz.

30 AUSCHWITZ

What did Auschwitz look like? Where was it located exactly? Who guarded it? Originally it had been an old Austrian-Hungarian barrack complex on the outskirts of the small town of Auschwitz, covering about six hectares. The red stone barracks were surrounded by a barrier of dual barbed wire.

The inside wires were live wires and there were a large number of watchtowers equipped with machine guns. 2.000 members of the SS, all carrying handguns, together with additional units of the Wehrmacht, were in charge of guarding the camp. Furthermore the camp was outfitted with 200 motorbikes, 25 cars and 35 trucks as well as two shortwave channels in case of emergency, such as a prisoner revolt. In that case the guards could immediately call for a garrison of members of the SS. There were about 30 guards for every 100 prisoners.

More than half of the prisoners were women. Fear, hunger and thirst ruled the camp. The majority of the prisoners weakened so quickly that after a short while the prisoners didn't even recognize each other anymore. They became apathetic and for many of them illness soon followed. From early 1941 until the spring of 1944 there were three typhus outbreaks that killed more than 10.000 prisoners.

The Dutch Jews seemed to be especially vulnerable. After all, they came from a beautiful, quiet and protected country, where most of them had had jobs, had earned a good living, in short had enjoyed a good life. In the camp they seemed to have shown less courage and soon were not themselves any longer. They thought everything was 'dirty' and hardly any of them spoke Yiddish, unlike the Polish Jews. Moreover very few of them spoke German, so they understood little of the German commands. The food was extremely bad, consisting of a piece of bread, awful-tasting coffee, and potatoes that were boiled down to mush or rather a runny soup. If they got anything at all! No one owned his or her own plate and it frequently happened that eight to ten people ate from one bowl.

Of course, many, if not most of them, understood that sooner or later they would be killed. The only question was 'how?' One could either end up in the gas chamber, be beaten or shot to death or commit suicide by simply running into the barbed wire. Many were 'abgespritzt', meaning they received a deadly injection to the heart. Others became seriously ill or died from exhaustion or malnutrition.

The first people to arrive in Auschwitz from Holland, among them my parents, suffered greatly. They were gassed in more primitive gas chambers than those who came later. The camp leadership was extremely cruel and especially the Dutch women suffered terribly and quickly became discouraged. Almost all suicides were committed by Dutch women. The Dutch Red Cross didn't do a single thing for the Dutch Jews. No one in Auschwitz ever received a single parcel.

People didn't want to aggravate the Germans. The Red Cross offered no help whatsoever to the Jews facing death. 'The Red Cross horribly failed to live up to its own principles,' said the former director Cees Breederveld. That statement was long overdue. Right after the war there were many complaints. Belgian, French and Norwegian citizens did receive packages with food from the Red Cross. And even after the war the Red Cross didn't offer any help to the Jews.

I have often wondered why the railroad tracks and the crematoria were never bombed. The Russians, the English and the Americans would, undoubtedly, have been capable of doing so. One of the excuses was that the gas chambers of the Sobibor complex were too far removed from the camp! Also, they didn't have any real precision bombs. As far as the Russians were concerned, everyone knew that Stalin was an outspoken anti-Semite. But the Allies surely would have been able to reach Auschwitz. The heavy bombers of the American Fifteenth Air Force, stationed in southern Italy since November, 1943, could easily have taken care of it. The town of Auschwitz was bombed twice, on July 21st and August 30th but sadly without the proper results.

You keep asking yourself over and over again why they didn't start bombing much earlier. One excuse could have been that during such bombing raids many innocent people could and would have been killed. How does this compare, however, with the thousands who were killed in the assembly lines?

Professor De Jong writes that England and Russia only reacted to this slaughter from a political point of view, without any human involvement. In 1944, America started to act more forcefully, but it was too late for many.

Generally speaking, the world let the Jews fend for themselves. Especially the Dutch government, as opposed to the Norwegian, the Danish and the Belgian authorities, didn't lift a finger.

31 MEANWHILE IN FRIESLAND

Meanwhile in Friesland the war continued. I became good friends with Dr. Minkema, the family doctor.

We had long conversations and he gave me some idea about what was happening in the big war on the outside. But I never found out the real truth.

The German soldiers hung around the farm more often, which meant that I had to hide in the chicken coup more than I cared to. One day Germans were swarming the farm. Beppe thought that they were coming to arrest Sjors and me, but instead they took all of us with them. We were forced to walk to the main road, where everybody in the village had gathered. The doctor, the grocery store owner, Sjoerd, Rein, Onne, Anne and even the minister. The whole village seemed to be present. After a while three cars arrived. There was a lot of yelling and name calling. Even though I couldn't understand it because it was all in German, I knew very well what was going on. Then I watched how Foppe de Haan was pulled from one of the cars. The doors of the other cars were opened as well and a total of twelve boys were pulled out. They were blindfolded and were put into a line.

Next I saw soldiers with rifles.

I remember how very quiet it suddenly became, except for the whistling of the birds. The minister began to pray while many of the onlookers started to cry. Then it happened. Shots were fired, very loud bangs rang out. I thought there were probably a hundred shots. All the men, boys still, fell to the ground, followed by yelling and screaming: 'That's what happens to traitors!'

Everybody was then allowed to return home, including Sjors and I.

Later that evening, in my bed, I learned the whole story. The farm of Foppe de Haan, called the 'terrorist farm' by the Germans, was being used by the resistance. In the cellar was a large hiding place with a printing machine and enough storage room for all sorts of material. In a moment of absent-mindedness someone had forgotten to close the hatch to the cellar. When German watchmen passed by that evening they noticed the light, which was forbidden anyhow for no light was allowed to show to the outside. When the Germans decided to have a closer look they discovered the cellar with the men, the printing equipment, weapons, food stamps and a lot more. They arrested all of them.

It was not until after the war that I found out what had happened. They weren't people from the 'terrorist farm' at all. Those people managed to escape from the Germans. It turned out to be innocent people that were arrested by the Germans as reprisal.

There are a lot of stories about what supposedly happened. This is one of the ones that is closest to the truth. On Thursday, April 29th, 1943 Fr. Christiansen announced that all Dutch soldiers had to be taken prisoners of war. They had previously been released by the Führer after the first crucial days in May 1940 as an act of generosity. After all they had been caught in the middle of anti-German activity, so they weren't allowed their freedom anymore.

The real reason, however, was that the German labor force was short of men. The solders revolted and there were strikes everywhere, in

Groningen and Friesland as well. The Germans did not want to end the strikes, which made immediate punishment lawful. The instructions were to hit marks during riots and gatherings. Rauter stated that it was not important to shoot the right people as long as there were deaths at the right moments.

A strike also took place in de Haar, an area between Marum and Frieschepalen near the Frisian-Groningen border. The next morning a German patrol car was driving along Haarsterweg. They had been expecting supplies for the German camp but had been victims of sabotage; the cars had been put out of order. It had made the soldiers very angry and the local commander decided to deal with it harshly.

He noticed a group of people standing in front of a farm. Hence, on that Monday morning sixteen young boys were arrested and imprisoned in a camp in Trimunt.

Major Johann Gerhard Mechels of the Grüne Polizei travelled personally from Groningen to investigate. He decided there would be no clemency for the saboteurs and gave the order to have all the young men executed. Guilty or not guilty was beside the point. Among those arrested was a thirteen-year-old boy.

The sentencing took place on a small hill near the south entrance of the camp. In the afternoon the men were forced outside and executed.

Along the road near Trimunt, and I still remember it, is a small monument that serves as a memorial of this tragedy. It reads: 'Died for their country as victims of the German terror on May 3rd, 1943. Berend Assies, Geert Jan Diertens, Jan and Karst Doornbosch, Johannes Glas, Andries, Dirk, Albert and Hendrik Hartholt, Eeuwe de Jong, Frits van de Riet, Gerrit van der Vaart, Sibbe de Wal, and Uitze, Jelle and Steven van de Wiel.'

After this event we were no longer allowed to play outside. Not even secretly. So I played inside or in the chicken coup. My health, thanks to the doctor and Beppe, did improve somewhat, but I remained a small, anxious little boy. I was far too small and too thin for my age. Without any concept of time, the days went by. Once a week I would go in the tub. When I was the first one, the water would still be warm; otherwise it would be cold and dirty. I was bored stiff. We obviously didn't have anything, no books or toys to keep us entertained. But I didn't know any better. I still had my wooden rabbit though.

The only real excitement came one evening when it started to rain hard, real hard. It was pitch-black outside and the rain came down like a heavy blanket. Beppe began packing a suitcase. Clothes, the Bible and some money. I had to sit on the suitcase to help close it. We had to make haste. Standing near the door we were waiting anxiously. The house had a straw roof and could easily be hit by lightening. The village had no fire department, which was the reason for the fear. I thought it was quite exciting, but of course nothing happened.

Some time later I suddenly received new clothes and a pair of yellow wooden shoes. I was finally allowed to go to school. Every morning we would walk through the cornfields to Drachtstercompagnie, where I learned how to do math and grammar and how to pray and to play.

I understood that the war had ended but for me everything continued as before, except that I no longer had to go into the chicken coup. I also learned to ice skate, using an old chair on the frozen ditch behind our house. I loved it so much!

32 THE END OF THE WAR

After five years the war had finally ended, a war which people once believed would last only a few weeks, maybe a few months.

We didn't know yet how the battle had gone down. In June of 1944 the Americans and English landed in Normandy. On August 24th of that year they liberated Paris and on September 3rd it was Brussels' turn. This meant that liberation would take place from the south.

On 'Dolle Dinsdag' the members of the NSB fled with all their worldly goods to The Hague, to the train station Hollandsch Spoor, from where 31 trains belonging to the Dutch Railway Company would transport about 40.000 NSB members and their families to Lüneburg in Germany. Sometime later, in early 1945, they were transported back to Groningen and Friesland in the Netherlands. During the final year of the war, misery was at its peak. In those parts of the country that had not yet been liberated, people suffered, mainly from hunger and the cold. During raids ten thousands of men and boys were arrested and carried off. In the western part of Holland 15.000 people died from starvation.

I never experienced hunger myself. Once in a while, in what was once the stable, Omke and Anne would slaughter a pig. I couldn't stand looking at it. First there were the awful screams and then all that blood. I didn't like the slaughter of chickens either. The cows survived, but I do remember that a number of them became ill. The veterinarian would be called, and he would examine the animal thoroughly. Not only would he shove his hand and arm in the cow's mouth but in the cow's rear end as well. The animal had foam all around its mouth. The men on the farm were told to urinate in a bottle. When the bottle was full, Anne or Omke opened the animal's mouth while the veterinarian dumped the content down the animal's throat. After a few days the animal would be miraculously cured and we would be able to drink the cow's milk again.

Members of the resistance were executed by the hundreds. There were many wild actions taken by members of the NSB and their cohorts. Mussert still collaborated with the occupying force; his men even fought against the advancing Allied troops. Then suddenly the trumpet sounded: Friesland was liberated, as the last province! This was in April 1945.

But was it really over?

Everywhere Jews and others left their hiding places. Most of them had literally lost everything: parents, children, family, home and property.

Finally I was allowed to play freely. I even went to school. Uncle Omke came home with a pair of new wooden clogs. Every morning I walked along the corn field, on my way to school with Rein. It was the first time and I was already ten years old!

The doctor visited the school one afternoon. He came to get me on his motorbike to take me home to Omke and Beppe. What happened next I will never forget. My Aunt Ju, my mother's sister, stood in the living room and suddenly we all became overwhelmed and began to cry. Everyone talked at once but there was also some whispering going on. Aunt Ju gave me a couple of big, wet kisses, which I did not like. I was bashful with all of these people around. Besides, since my parents had left, I had never had a kiss and here was Aunt Ju constantly kissing me. We had dinner and shortly after Aunt Ju – 'Juutje' as she was called – left again. I was totally confused and wasn't quite sure what was going to happen to me next. Why did Aunt Ju leave? Would I ever see her again?

That evening I had to go to bed early, but of course I couldn't sleep. A movie kept playing inside my head. What was my real name? Did I have to leave this place too? Would I now see my father and mother again?

33 THE NIGHTMARE

At night I would dream and my screams would wake everybody up. The night after seeing Aunt Ju again, when I finally woke up from my nightmare, Beppe, Omke and the doctor were standing by my bedside. I was completely confused and my whole body had turned yellow.

The doctor's diagnosis was acute jaundice caused by anxiety. It probably happened because he saw his aunt again, Beppe said, and kept holding my hand. Together we prayed that my health would return. The pastor also came to visit. 'Japje, the war is over. Everybody has now been liberated. Your Uncle Louis and Aunt Ju have survived the horror as well as your cousin Etty. They are all living in Amsterdam again.'

I remember that conversation very clearly, although I didn't understand what it was all about. I also remember that he said at the end: 'They would also like you to come to Amsterdam and live with them.'

I broke down in a terrible crying fit and suddenly became scared, very scared. What would be happening to me now again? Wasn't this, after all, my home, with Beppe and Omke? They contacted the principal, who explained everything to me. About Hitler and the Germans, the collaborators, the resistance and the people in hiding. He also told me that I never had to fear being taken away from Beppe and Omke. After all I was a real Frisian little boy!

After a while I began to recover, no more fever and no more yellow skin. My crying spells started to diminish as well. The only thing that did not go away was the asthma, in spite of the many powders and pills. I returned to school and slowly things began to look more normal.

But that wouldn't last long.

One Thursday morning I had to stay home from school and I watched Beppe packing a bag. With my clothes! Her eyes filled up with tears when she told me that we would be going to Amsterdam, to Aunt Ju and Uncle Louis. I didn't have to be afraid because they were going with me. That evening everyone came to say goodbye, including the doctor and the pastor. I felt awful and was struck by panic again. What was going to happen to me now?

34 BACK TO AMSTERDAM

After a long journey by boat and train we finally arrived at the central station in Amsterdam, where Aunt Ju and Etty, now called Tet, were waiting for us. Streetcar 25 took us to Biesboschstraat. It was a peculiar ride, all those people and all that traffic. Besides, I didn't understand a word, I only spoke Frisian now. Still it was strangely exciting because I didn't know a thing beyond Ureterp, Drachtstercompagnie and Drachten.

When we arrived at Biesboschstraat 50, we had to walk up two sets of stairs. When we entered the house there was an entrance hall, two beautiful rooms, two bedrooms, a kitchen, a toilet and even a bathroom... it looked like a hotel! I had never seen anything like it.

'And this is your room, Salo,' Aunt Ju said. No box-bed but a foldaway bed and a sink, attached to the wall. Electric light, but no pets. I started to transpire profusely. Everybody seemed so busy and all the neighbors wanted to meet Salo. 'He is a small, delicate little boy,' I heard someone say, but I didn't know what to make of it. Beppe and Omke stayed and slept in the attic room at their request.

During the first few days at Biesboschstraat, we visited all the neighbors and acquaintances. Fortunately Omke and Beppe joined me. After a few days, however, they suddenly left. It was on a Wednesday. They had me sit on their lap and explained to me that it would be better for them to return home again. After all, this was the place where I belonged, with my family. They would always love me. I had to learn to speak well and attend a good school. I would be welcome to spend every vacation with them.

I felt desperate to be left suddenly by the people dearest to me in the whole world. Crying and filled with anger I held on to Beppe. They could not leave me with these people, who I could not even understand all that well and hardly knew. I wanted to return with Beppe and Omke. I had to return with them.

Unfortunately, Beppe and Omke left, leaving me behind, terrified. I was left all alone in Amsterdam, no Beppe, no Omke, and no friends. I was not allowed outside by myself and no one spoke Frisian. That's how my days went by. I slept poorly, refused to eat, and cried a lot. And there was always that fear. I began to stammer.

35 ASTHMA, BASED ON A NERVOUS CONDITION

Again, I became ill. I was often short of breath. There wasn't any powder available for my inhaler from the market in Friesland. A strange doctor came to pay a visit. His name was Baader, his diagnosis: 'Asthma based on a nervous condition.' Where were Beppe and Omke? Where was Dr. Minkema? I felt abandoned! Certainly there were aunts visiting me: Stella, Bep, Guurtje, Lena, Nettie and Settie.

I seemed to be a sickly, nervous and scared little boy, who was far too small for his age. Aunt Ju took me to all kinds of doctors, good ones and bad ones, as I would later understand. In the meantime I received lessons in the Dutch language from a very strict woman. They were actually elocution lessons. 'You have to pay attention, Salo,' she would constantly say. I also had difficulty with 'Salo', I was, after all, used to people calling me 'Japje'. I was also being pampered in a way totally foreign to me.

One evening Aunt Ju told me that my parents were dead. They had been gassed by the Germans in Poland. I didn't want to believe it. Hadn't I been taught in Friesland that if you wanted something, you should pray to God? That He would help you? And that's how I started to pray secretly every evening before I went to sleep. Hours on end. 'If it is Your will, then please let my papa and mama return to me.' After all, other people had returned.

But not my father and mother. Why not? What had they done to deserve this? What had I done? I saw it then and I still see it today, the sight of my parents on the stage in the Schouwburg, and not being allowed to go to them. Me, crying for a week in the daycare facility. They left without me, their son.

I refused to eat and the shortness of breath got worse. I missed Beppe and Omke every day, but I gradually began to feel at home with Aunt Ju and Uncle Louis. I hoped I would be allowed to stay there. And that was indeed the case, even if it took a lot of effort. The court had to approve this arrangement. Like so many other orphans from the war, I was originally supposed to be put in the orphanage Bergstichting in Laren, but Ju and Louis managed to get approval to take me in. Uncle Louis became my guardian. Out of respect for my parents, they didn't want to adopt me. 'You are and will always be a Muller.' Their name was Menist.

36 BIRTHDAY

Suddenly I had a birthday! I had totally forgotten that there was such a thing as my birthday. On March 1st, 1946 – February 29th did not appear on the calendar that year because it was not a leap year – we celebrated my birthday for the first time together: I had turned ten. It was a room full of sad people. Everyone was waiting for one or the other family member who might yet return. I, too, belonged to those that were waiting. Had my prayers been in vain?

Still, this birthday became an unforgettable one for me. I suddenly got gifts, even my first watch. Unfortunately I couldn't wear it because my wrist was too thin and it kept falling off. Aunt Ju had baked a butter cake, the best one ever. Nobody has ever been able to bake a better butter cake!

Time brought rest. I learned how to speak Dutch quite well and was less afraid. Just when I began to really feel at home with my 'new' papa, mama and little sister, something terrible happened.

On the advice of doctors, who 'know everything', I was told to spend some time In Switzerland, where I would improve greatly. It would do me a lot of good and help with the asthma. What a mistake! How could those doctors, who I assume should have had some insight into psychology, give such advice?

Since I was Jewish, something I never thought about, a search began for a Jewish foster home in Luzern. Great! They found one quite quickly. With a large group of kids, I left Amsterdam. I was screaming and crying when they put me on the train. I didn't stop crying until we reached Basel; it reminded me of the time I was separated from my parents.

We stayed overnight in Basel where I experienced my second nightmare. We were sleeping in a large, dark room on very small cots. I thought I had to use the bathroom and got out of bed. It was not until hours later our guides found me somewhere in the hallway of the old school where we were spending the night. The guides never left my side, afraid that something would happen to me again. I guess they felt sorry for me.

Finally, after what seemed like days, we arrived in Luzern. My new foster parents were fairly young, Orthodox Jews who spoke Swiss German, a dialect generally spoken in that part of Switzerland. I didn't understand them, which meant that we could not communicate. Again, I felt alone.

37 DREAMS ABOUT MY DECEASED PARENTS

My foster parents tried to soften my sorrow. Every day, after returning home from the office, my stepdad would hand me a couple of new postage stamps, which I glued into an album. On Saturday I went to synagogue. Here, too, everybody was very nice to me, even though I couldn't understand what they were saying.

One night I dreamed about my dead father. He was sitting in a chair in a small empty room. He looked like a skeleton and played the accordion. The sick feeling that came over me lasted a number of weeks and I couldn't tell anyone about it. Each night I feared that I would have another nightmare. To this day, I think about this dream.

In Luzern I watched a man and a woman kiss for the first time. During the war I had never seen people kiss one another, let alone that someone would have kissed me. It always happened in the afternoon, after teatime, on the sofa in the living room. It was not my foster parents, no, it was my foster father and the maid!

While they thought I was focusing on my postage stamps, they crawled on the sofa together. I would sneak to the door, anxious to find out what they were doing. One afternoon I noticed that my foster father had taken off the maid's panties and that he had started to kiss her and lick her between her legs. Shocked, I suddenly started to cough. They jumped off the sofa as if stung by a bee and locked me up in a room. From the sounds I could tell that they were finishing what they had started. Actually, it wasn't all that strange to me. On the farm I had often watched when horses and cows were being impregnated. I've seen these things in a brothel many times as well. Following this incident, my foster father treated me even better. Every day he brought a gift for me. The maid paid more attention to me as well. She took me outside and I was allowed to join her when she went grocery shopping. She also taught me German from a picture book and consequently I kept learning more words.

The shortness of breath became worse, however. The doctor thought it better for me to leave Luzern. It was damp and not at a high enough altitude.

Every day people came to see me and every day the doctor came to listen to my lungs. It was decided that I had to go to Davos, where the air was dry and healthy. Sehr gut für Salomon!

38 CHILDREN'S HOME VILLA JENNY

One Wednesday morning an unknown woman came to get me and take me to the children's home Villa Jenny in Davos, where young children, specifically those with lung problems, were housed. They had come from all over, except from the Netherlands. Again, I wasn't able to talk to anyone. I had to share my room with a boy from England who was older and much taller than me.

Another disaster occurred. Villa Jenny was a large house with children and nurses who I couldn't understand. There were very strict rules. We weren't allowed anything. We had to ask for everything and everything started exactly on time. We had to get up at seven and were forced to urinate, even if we didn't have to. Next, it was back to bed for 'lung exercise'. We had to lie on our stomach in such a way that our legs were still on the bed but our hands were reaching the floor. Next we had to cough until the mucus in our lungs had loosened enough that we were able to cough it up and spit it out in a jar. The nurses kept checking and if there wasn't enough you had to continue coughing.

Once you had succeeded you were allowed to go to the dining room 'as a reward'. There we had to wait until everyone was present. Each time they would announce the name of the person we were still waiting for. I tried very hard but wasn't able to cough up enough mucus each time. As punishment I had to help dry the dishes. However, if you had done well, which happened rarely, you got dessert: chocolate mousse with whipped cream.

By nine o'clock we were ready for our sports lessons. Sport was the most important thing it seemed. We were taught to stand up for ourselves. Skating, skiing, sledding and walking were required. Then back by eleven for language classes. After that we had a warm lunch until one thirty. I had to rest from two until four o'clock since they still considered me too sick and weak to do other things.

During those hours I had to lie outside on the balcony on a stretcher, while the door behind me was closed. It became very quiet in- and outside the house. I hated it. I had panic attacks and had to use the toilet frequently, but that was not allowed so I often wet my pants, even at eleven years old. Every day I was dreading the afternoon. Actually, anxiety made me need to use the toilet the moment the door fell shut behind me. Sometimes I was able to hold it for a couple of hours but after that I had to run inside to the toilet.

Then one day, I really couldn't hold it any longer and decided to urinate over the balcony into the snow, leaving a yellow trail. This, of course, was discovered and I was called to the office of the director. She was a nasty and strict woman with black hair and big breasts, which she continually pressed against me.

But this time I was able to understand her reasonably well. How did I have the nerve to urinate over the balcony! I didn't show any sign of remorse but explained to her that I couldn't hold it any longer. I hadn't been a good boy and therefore had to dry dishes for a whole week without a reward. I was no longer permitted to rest on the balcony and received extra ski lessons.

Months passed and during that time I was taught how to cough, sleep and especially how to be obedient. In fact, I didn't learn a thing, or if I did it was definitely to do with skiing, which kept us occupied for hours each day.

39 COLLECTING POSTAGE STAMPS

If we had behaved, at least in the eyes of the school mistress, we were allowed to do something of our own choosing. When I left Luzern I received a stamp collection so I could trade stamps. I had to ask first, and I had to show the stamps and mention with whom I wanted to trade. My roommate, Jim, had not traded 'truthfully', which meant drying dishes, three days in a row. One Saturday we were to try our hands at working with clay. We were all given a piece of soft clay with the assignment to make something from it, a house, a skier, a boy, a girl, a car or even yourself. You were not allowed to copy. I tried my very best and made a little man on skis.

After a thorough inspection by the mistress I was awarded the second price: chocolate mousse with whipped cream after dinner. My happiness was short-lived. When the mistress walked into our room for the inspection, we were no longer allowed to touch our projects. She snarled that she didn't want to know who had made what. In his enthusiasm Jim wanted to straighten his project a little bit. Unfortunately, the mistress noticed it. She grabbed his little clay man and kneaded it into a ball. 'You always need to listen, Jim! Go to your room. I don't want to see you anymore.' Jim walked away in tears. He would have won first prize for sure but now he had to dry dishes.

Every day I asked myself why I didn't hear anything from Aunt Ju. I also asked the mistress but she never answered me. No one paid attention when, in February, my birthday came around, but I guess I had gotten used to that by now. Much later, after I had returned to Biesboschstraat in Amsterdam with Aunt Ju, I learned that she had sent me a postcard every week. She had even called me on my birthday but they had refused to let me talk on the phone. It would have made me nervous and 'homesickness' was supposed to be over by now. What did the mistress mean by that? After all, I didn't have a home any longer. I only missed the people I had gotten to know such as Beppe, Omke, Ju and Louis and maybe Etty too.

After a few months, I started to calm down again. Or did it only seem like it? Whatever the case, I suddenly had to leave, away from Davos and Villa Jenny. Bye mistress, Jim, Anna, Greetje, Walter, Heinrich and all the others. Salo was on his way again.

When I arrived at the central station in Amsterdam Aunt Ju and my cousin Tet were waiting for me. Tears and hugs again. They had missed me terribly but they had not been allowed to be in contact with me. That's why I hadn't heard from them.

I got my own bedroom back with the foldaway bed and a wash basin of my own.

40 EATING VOMIT TO LEARN A LESSON

I wasn't doing well. I was a small, scared little boy that was still suffering from asthma. Davos hadn't helped at all. Aunt and Uncle were having a difficult time with me. I was too scared to stay at home alone. If they wanted to go out, they had to find a sitter for me. My cousin – I would start calling her my sister later – had a difficult time too, since my presence demanded a lot of attention. Luckily she was much less damaged from living in hiding during the war than I was. She was lucky enough to have stayed with her mother the whole time. Her father, whom she had had to call Uncle Henk, stayed somewhere else in the same village, Nederhorst den Berg.

I remained very anxious, I was stuttering and constantly asked if I was lovable. Why I did that I don't know. Maybe people didn't really like me. And I didn't mean anything to them and their own children were nicer. Maybe I just really wanted to hear that I was a good boy.

The dream I had in Luzern kept coming back to me. I didn't dare to tell anyone about it and I was afraid that it would come back when I went to sleep; I could barely sleep. I started sleepwalking and became irritable. I didn't want to eat anymore. I just couldn't do it. Aunt Ju, whom I was allowed to call mama, did everything to help me. She even started feeding me. It took hours before I had even remotely finished my plate. I kept big chunks of food in my mouth and secretly spat them out in the toilet. It became so bad that my aunt often lost her patience. Once, she dumped an entire plate of pink pudding on my head. After dinner I would frequently throw up. Dr. Fiedeldij Dop recommended that I should start eating my vomit and that would teach me not to do it. Even that didn't help. It took years before I starting eating normally again.

Going to school was a mess too. In the beginning I was put in a class with children that were four or five years younger than me, although you couldn't really tell at first. I was small, fragile and walked with a crooked back from the asthma. On top of that, the stuttering kept getting worse. The school directors insisted this wasn't because of my anxiety, but because I was left-handed. I was taught to leave that behind me, because it wasn't proper. Neatly write everything with your right hand. That was hard to do at first as well.

With my mama I visited all the doctors that might be able to help find relief for my ever-worsening asthma and anxiety. I remember a whole lot of them: Baader, Levie, Bosman in The Hague and the Allergie-Kliniek in Emmastraat in Amsterdam. Drs. Van der Bijl and Van der Werff spent hours with me there. Until I ended up at Professor Groen's.

He treated me as a serious victim of war and told people that they were supposed to take that into account. The diets of the allergists were thrown in the trash and I was allowed to eat anything I wanted. That was a surprise. Especially a lot of chocolate, cheese, eggs and milk.

Against everyone's expectations I started growing quickly and my asthma got a little better. I also became more confident. I was moved up two years in school, though that was still two years below the grade I was supposed to be in. That wasn't easy, but with some hard work I ended up in the third grade of the Dongeschool.

41 AMERICAN CHEWING GUM

'It wouldn't do anyone any good if Salo, at eleven years of age, would be put in the first grade,' the principal, Mr. R.H. Zandvoort, said. And thus it didn't happen. My parents always followed the advice of others such as doctors, psychologists, teachers, friends, neighbors, the man who sold pickles, the poultry farmer, the soda salesman, the cheese farmer, the butcher and even strangers.

I was tutored daily. I ended up in the third grade in a class with, I thought, only annoying boys and girls. Here, my severe asthma was a huge handicap as well. I was wondering what I was doing there. What did they want from me? I was little, stuttered, wore glasses and had lost eight years of my life. But I looked nice. My father always brought the nicest sweaters home from the store. My hair looked neat because of the pomade I used daily in large quantities. Despite everything I was able to make friends quickly. I was fortunate that I had a distant aunt living in America who regularly sent care packages including, among other things, coffee and Wrigley chewing gum. The gum was of good use to me, since I was able to 'buy' numerous friends that way. At school they almost killed me for a piece of chewing gum once. A boy from one of the higher grades wanted a piece. I refused. He then grabbed me from behind and began to strangle me. When I fell to the ground, almost unconscious, he pulled a chewed piece of gum from my mouth and stuck it in his own. I came to with the assistance of the gym teacher.

My chewing gum made up for a lot. Later on I would exchange it for marbles. I carried pockets full of them and everybody wanted to play with me. I was also the only one in my class who owned a leather soccer ball. My pride and joy! All the boys wanted to join me in a game of soccer. Due to my asthma I was always the goaltender. You didn't have to do much and there was definitely no running. During lunchtime when I had to eat at home, which I didn't like, I had my 'friends' keep the ball. Back at school, one day, I immediately noticed that something was wrong. Nobody said a word. Then I saw it. My ball, my gem, my pride was punctured. Like a small, sad pile, it was lying on the floor next to my desk. At lunchtime they had started throwing the ball around. Ton de Bruin had caught it with his dip pen. Wham, flat, no longer usable. For years I would walk past sporting goods stores to see if I could find a ball like the one I had, but I never was able to locate one.

My school years went by with many ups and downs. Often I had to stand in the corner. Having Mr. Lauman pull my ear became normal for me. My mother would just say, 'You probably deserved it.' Most often that was indeed the case.

I remained difficult: at school and for myself. I still missed my own parents very much and was still hoping for their return. After all, quite a few people had 'suddenly' showed up, people who had been thought to have died. In spite of all my prayers my parents never returned. Would there ever be anyone who understood what that meant to me? Would I ever be able to get through this, even with the love I received from Ju and Louis? The love, care and sacrifices they made actually became a burden to me. It was as if a claim had been put upon me and I continued my 'war' habits. I tried to be a very good boy, which was not difficult since I had got used to it. The result was, however, that at school I found myself between a rock and a hard place. I had difficulty concentrating, remained anxious and often got into trouble because of my big mouth. After all, being the oldest in the class I was supposed to set a good example.

In spite of all this I still passed. I began to think about my future. What would I like to be? What was best for Salo?

I saw less and less of Beppe and Omke. My father was back with De Vries van Buuren. Along with a few remaining former colleagues and a generation of new colleagues, they tried to rebuild the business. They worked day and night. Although he didn't have a good command of foreign languages, he would travel to eastern Europe for weeks on end to buy textiles. My mother, too, had to work very hard to make ends meet. This often led to tension and disagreements. The result was that my father sacrificed his job and became a textile representative. He got a car, and carried eight suitcases with which he made his daily visits to various shopkeepers. Every morning the suitcases had to be carried downstairs and then back upstairs in the evening, but it was a lot better than those long-distance trips, for Ju, Tet and myself as well. My father's schedule did not leave enough time to visit Beppe and Omke in Friesland.

Eventually I was finally to spend my vacation with them, riding my bike. Sjors was coming along and he and I left early in the morning. The asthma made it difficult. When we arrived it was dark and we could not find the little house. After searching for hours someone showed us the way and at last we arrived, in the middle of the night. Again I had to sleep in the box-bed. They still used water from the well and the restroom with the pages from the Psalms was still called 'het huuske', but they now had electricity and radio reception. The house was still damp and dusty and as a result I had a severe asthma attack. There was instant panic. Nobody knew what to do, even the doctor was at a loss. I had to go back to Amsterdam and of course not by bike. I was taken to the train station by horse and wagon and arrived late at night at the central station in Amsterdam, feeling sicker than a dog. Again, Ju was waiting for me. Back home in Biesboschstraat, the doctor gave me a Multergan injection and a couple of days later I began to feel better again.

There was no way I would be able to go back to Friesland. Beppe, whose real name was Pietje Heddema-Bos, died on September 6th, 1958. She was put to rest in de Kniepe. Omke, known as Klaas Vellinga, followed her four years later on August 20th, 1962. His burial place was in Houtige Hage. It seemed they had never married and were thus not allowed to be buried next to each other. I thought this was terrible. They were such great, kind people. Imagine the courage they demonstrated to take in two difficult Jewish boys during the war. Still, I was never grateful at the time for what they did. That came much later. I succeeded, with the help of Rein, in getting the distinguished Yad Vashem award for them. It wasn't an easy process. An application is sent to The Holocaust Martyrs' and Heroes' Remembrance Authority in Jerusalem. They need to know everything about the people for whom you're requesting the award. Eventually the story in this book was the deciding factor. On November 15th, 2007 I received a letter that stated that the Commission for Designation of the Righteous has decided to award the title of 'Righteous Among the Nations' to Pietje Heddema-Bos and to Klaas Vellinga, for the help rendered to Jewish people during the period of the Holocaust at the risk of their lives. It was definitely at the risk of their own lives.

Through the embassy in The Hague I handed over the award during a special ceremony in the Jewish Historical Museum, in the presence of Omke and Beppe's grandchildren. I was also allowed to announce that their names had been added to 'The Wall of Honor' at Yad Vashem. It was a special and emotional day for me. They so deserved it.

42 WHY DID I SURVIVE?

With the passing of the years it became more and more difficult for me to deal with my problems. I often thought: why did I survive? Was I happy about it? When I was looking at old pictures taken at parties I saw at least eighty family members. I was the only one left. What a lucky man!

I considered every day a sacrifice.

I expected a lot of myself and everything had to be done just right. In addition to doing my homework I also had to do the grocery shopping. After all, my father and mother worked. When I grumbled, I was told: 'We have done so much for you, it will not hurt you to do something for us.' That was the feeling I had right from the beginning when I moved in with my new parents. Throughout the years, until the death of Louis in 1985 and Ju in 1992, I have fulfilled the duties of a good son, not only with great effort but also with love. I was always there for them. I planned my vacations in such a way that they were never alone. New Year's Eve was celebrated together. My parents came first, and then my own family. They had always supported me, after all.

Actually, I never had problems with my father. Louis was a quiet, kind man who had also lost his whole family during the war. His brother, Ab, a member of the resistance, was executed early on. He never wanted to talk about it.

I did clash with my mother sometimes. She meddled in everything and was overly fretful. But that was out of love. She did everything for her sister Lena, my real mother. Early in the war they had come to an agreement that if one of them would not survive, the other one would take care of the child.

I was the child and Ju became the mother. She never forgave herself for the fact that she had survived and that she hadn't been able to do anything for her sister, brother-in-law and parents.

Quite often the question was raised: 'What is Salo planning to be when he grows up?' I did know the answer: doctor. I needed to be tested. Lawyer, doctor or teacher. Those were the recommendations of the experts. That's how I ended up going to Het Amsterdams Lyceum, Mr. Gunning's school.

43 DEPARTURE FROM MY RELIGION

In the meantime I had turned 13 years old, a very special age for Jewish boys. What to do? During the war I had interacted with different religions. One family made me join them each Sunday morning in a Catholic church and again in the afternoon. Occasionally a wafer was put on my tongue. With another family, I had to go to Sunday school classes held by a minister. But, no matter how fiercely I prayed, my parents never returned. I became so angry and so sad that I refused to become bar mitzvah. The fact that I would be receiving a lot of gifts could not alter my thoughts. I was done with religion. To this day I cannot bring myself to go to synagogue, not even on Yom Kippur. If I feel the need to meditate, I do that at home, alone or in the presence of my wife. I do go to the monument at the Apollolaan every year on May 4th with my wife, children and the eldest grandchildren. Although I find it difficult, I consider it a duty. Everybody is remembered on that day. Without drawn-out sermons or smooth words.

And thus my 13th birthday was celebrated at a small gathering of friends and neighbors. My parents got me a beautiful bicycle. A beautiful BSA. My aunt gave me a carrier for my bike. My only uncle treated me to a box of rum bonbons.

Aunt Ju and Uncle Louis were never able to accept the fact that this uncle and aunt, a sister and brother of my (real) father, had been able to obtain a 'sper', without consideration for their brother and sister-in-law. Ju was never able to talk to her as before. Besides, she was very disturbed that they had never shown any interest in me. After the war, my parents went through difficult times financially. To pay the medical bills pertaining to my asthma they even had to sell some of their jewelry. But the aunt and uncle never even tried to find out if they could possibly do something for Salo, their brother's only remaining child. Later, when I was about fifteen years old, I visited them quite frequently. They also lived in Biesboschstraat like us, with my cousins Aby and Sonja.

I discovered that sometimes things just happen that way. But fortunately not everyone acts like that.

Going to Het Amsterdams Lyceum was probably the best education anyone could receive. My parents had to buy a stock in the school for me to be able to attend. This was no problem for them. After all, I was the son of Ju's sister.

Mr. Gunning had been good during the occupation, and the teachers had refused to sign the Aryan declaration at the start of the war. Names of the students who never returned have been engraved in the school's auditorium for a lasting memorial.

The first two years I worked really hard. I wanted to prove that I could do well. But again, I was the oldest in my class. And I also wanted to do more than just learn. That was allowed, but only after I had finished my homework. I joined the school rowing club De Drietand. And apparently I could play a fair game of field hockey. I was even allowed to sign up for a real club. But I was rejected by the Hockey Club Amsterdam. My father was not the type of man they were accustomed to having around at this club. He was only a salesman, so they didn't give me a chance. Or maybe it was because I was Jewish?

The nice, quiet and sickly little boy gradually became a rebellious, spiteful and sad student. I preferred play over study. Besides, my mother wasn't home much, since she worked in the fabric shop of Jacques Snoek on Nieuwendijk four days a week. This meant that no one was home when I returned home from school, so I stopped doing my homework. I preferred to draw or play outside. The teachers started to complain, they wanted to take action. I had to do my homework under supervision. That's how I got to know Mrs. Flach, a kind, somewhat older lady who had once been a teacher. With her help I passed and started the third grade.

44 SCHOOL: A MESS

But somehow things went wrong anyway. I couldn't find the energy to fully concentrate on my studies. I wanted to do other things. For six years I hadn't been able to do what other children had been allowed to do. I just had to be quiet and good. This took its toll on me eventually.

Through tutoring, plenty of supervision, and some tricks from the teachers I managed to keep up. One of my classmates, Dick Polet, a great guy, gave me a lot of support. He helped me with my homework. During lunchtime we often went to his home in Witte de Withstraat. He had very sweet parents, and a sister called Bettie. These people gave me advice and helped in any way they could.

I became class representative and took care of the class register. When one of my classmates had misbehaved I had to defend them before the principal and the teachers: I became the 'school lawyer'. I loved it. I would brag and everybody was in awe of me. Everybody meaning the students. The teachers found me indolent and impertinent.

For instance, I had problems with Mr. Kuijk, who taught Dutch. He was a very arrogant individual who always knew best. On the other hand, my English teacher, Mr. Texeira de Matos, tutored me on Saturday morning. And Mr. Beets, our homeroom teacher who also taught geography, helped when and wherever I needed it. I also had a good rapport with my chemistry teacher. He would frequently bum a cigarette from me. However, all the other teachers were against me, so I was held back and had to repeat third grade.

My parents were asked to come and see our new principal, Mr. Van den Broek, a brusque, cold and unkind person who had showed no understanding for my situation. 'Salo has to go to another school. He can no longer stay with us,' he said.

People began to think. And again they asked: 'What will be best for Salo?'

Due to all the worries my health worsened. My parents tried everything to get my asthma attacks under control. I visited an army of doctors with my mother, such as Dr. Gerrits and Dr. Noach. Dr. Gerrits, who had a practice in Waldeck Pyrmontlaan, kept encouraging me. Sadly he was hit by a streetcar and died in the hospital. Then it was Dr. Noach's turn. He recognized my problem straight away. He was a miracle worker and I received new medication. Initially I used large inhalers that were difficult to carry around. Later they were replaced by smaller ones. I still carry one with me. Four inhalations daily along with my medication.

45 SUMMER SEX EDUCATION

During the summer we always went to Bergen, where my parents rented a big villa. Everyone could join: my cousin Leo, his sister Meta, Loes, the daughter of good friends of my parents as well her gorgeous cousin Truus, Edith and Pien and Joop as well as Victor and Betty.

The girls, Pien in particular, taught me my first 'sex lessons'.

Later on we exchanged the town of Bergen for Noordwijk. Again everyone joined. At times the asthma attacks became so bad that Pien carried me on her back for hours, or I had to be seated on the carrier of her bike.

Every year the vacations were great fun. Plans were made months ahead of time. I also remember the vacations in Ellekom and Evolène in Switzerland really well. In Ellekom my parents rented the house of the grammar school principal. During the evenings we would sneak into the school. There was an organ in one of the classrooms, and we played it for hours on end, until my mother intervened.

My mother and my cousin Meta had a bicycle accident in Ellekom. Every day we set off on bike rides with me seated on the carrier. The woods were beautiful and riding along very narrow paths we always found our way. One day my mother hit a branch and was launched into the air. She finally came to a standstill under her bike. She didn't move. Minutes later our screams had woken her up. All of us carried her home. The next day she could only sit. She had bruises all over. She never rode her bike after that out of fear.

My asthma attacks kept shaping me life. I wasn't allowed to smoke of course. But I would still do it secretly sometimes!

Our family doctor, Dr. Levie, moved to Apeldoorn. Dr. Cardozo became his successor. He was an older and slightly grumpy man. He was a typical old-fashioned family doctor. Dr. Levie advised me to go see his neighbor, Dr. Arnold Weijel, a great guy. He was available day and night. He pulled me through several bouts of depression. Every Saturday morning I went to see him at the Binnengasthuis hospital to talk to him for an hour. That man helped me tremendously.

Aunt Jo, related by marriage to Uncle Bram, passed away from a wasting sickness, leaving Uncle Bram to take care of five children. My mother decided to take care of the family and thus the four of us moved to Albrecht Dürerstraat. Despite the loss of their mother, their lives continued in a happy way. I shared a room with my cousin Leo, which we very much enjoyed. My oldest cousin, Felix, had a job while the other cousins, Herman and Bernard, like their sister Meta, were still in school.

I loved it at Uncle Bram's house. At last I could play freely. During dinnertime Uncle Bram would tell the most wonderful stories about the olden days in old Jewish Amsterdam, about people he had known and of course about the war.

46 SALO, THE NUISANCE

All my male cousins suffered from asthma. They had gotten used to the illness, the attacks and the medication. At least at my cousins' house I wasn't an exception. Herman, Bernard and Leo went to the nicest and best school in Amsterdam, the Tweede OHS (Second Public Commercial School), while their sister Meta went to an inferior girls' high school. I liked the stories I heard about the OHS. But would they accept me? Salo, the troublesome boy? A long discussion between my parents and the principal removed the last barriers. The next semester I would be joining the third grade of the OHS.

I was placed in classroom 3A, the same room as my cousin Leo. The first day I entered the classroom the teacher told me to get seated in the first row near the door. 'And Leo, please take a seat at the other side of the room.' My reputation had gotten ahead of me.

A wonderful time followed. The teachers were very kind and I made new friends. I had Miss Muller in geography, Mr. Van der Knoop in English, Mr. Van Straaten in history, Mr. Van Duuren in political science, Mr. Veldman in economics and Mr. Karsten in Dutch literature. He always rewarded my essays with a 9. 'You're a good writer, Salo.' I still see those teachers standing in front of the class.

Except for my asthma my life seemed to be going in the right direction. I had a lot of homework but it was great to be going to the OHS together with my cousins. Karel de Wolf became my closest friend. Every day he would come over to the house and he would join us on our vacations. He became a sort of brother.

After a while we returned to our own home since Uncle Bram had hired a housekeeper, Miss Fien. I still see her once in a while. My mother returned to work and suddenly I found myself alone at home after school. Supervision and routine went out the window and I went back to my old ways. Karel helped me as much as he could, let me cheat and did a lot of my homework. Things started to go wrong in school. Again my parents were called in for a talk. 'So once in a while Salo also skips school.' I had even gone as far as to forge my father's signature. My mother decided to quit her job in order to assist me with my homework. That worked out really well. Until deep in the night we practiced French, English and German words and learned them by heart, also memorizing all of the grammar. I knew my history book from cover to cover.

I began having girlfriends: Juup, Maaike, Rietje, Wil, Helen, Nel, Joyce and Louise. I also became editor of the school newspaper *Het Kompas* with Bert and Jaap. But unfortunately I wasn't able to keep it together. After fifth grade everything turned sour again.

I was tested again. The results were the same: doctor, teacher or lawyer.

'But what would Salo like to become?'

'A doctor.'

'In that case you have to finish school.'

But that was no longer an option. Compared to the other students I was too old. They looked up to me: Salo isn't afraid of anything, he talks back to the teachers and doesn't take any dirt from anyone. At the same time, however, I wanted to help people and knew how to solve each and every problem. But one thing I couldn't do and that was to help myself.

Because of their worries about me, my father and mother began to neglect Tet. She became ill. The doctors weren't able to find out what exactly was wrong with her but a psychiatrist thought it wise to have her leave home for a year. And thus my sister – cousin – set out for Amersfoort with a suitcase full of clothing. It appeared that she was suffering from Cushing's Syndrome. Luckily she returned home after a year, fully recovered. We had a nice time together, even more so because of the friends she had made at the university. She, too, still suffered from the aftermath of the war. To be with strangers, even with your mother there, for four long years and not be allowed to do anything except chores was not the right way to live for a young child.

So I had to leave school again. There was no other way. But what to do next? Where would I end up? Fill shelves at the grocery store De Gruyter? Butcher boy or errand boy?

'You tell us, Salo, we've run out of ideas. We have done everything we can, but if someone isn't willing then there is not much left for us to do. Why don't you go and find yourself a job?'

There I was. Of course I had no idea either. The stuttering had become worse and so had my asthma. I was able to get a job with Philip Brothers, a trading firm. It didn't interest me at all. I would be taught commerce, but I had to learn to speak English perfectly. There was also the opportunity for me to be sent abroad. The latter option I didn't like at all. I would be removed from home again, staying with strangers. I didn't want to think about it.

47 A SHORT FUSE

I went to the employment office. 'What can I do for you?' the lady asked. Did I really know what I wanted? They had a job for me with Ambachtsheer and Van der Meulen at the timber docks. I would learn everything there was to learn about lumber. My parents didn't want to come along. They figured it was time for me to grow up. Thus, I got on my bike to the docks at the end of Spaarndammerstraat. I had taken an extra puff to not arrive sounding asthmatic.

Ambachtsheer and Van der Meulen, a long-standing and well-known company, were importers of lumber for contractors. There were five people working at the office and eighty at the lumberyard, all typically born and raised in Amsterdam. I was received by Mr. Van Bruggen, a kind but somewhat nervous person. They would train me to become an assistant business manager and I got my own desk and telephone. He introduced me to the Misters Ambachtsheer. They were old-fashioned gentlemen in dark suits and very formal. They dealt with the hardwood, used for furniture, windowsills and doors. 'Knock first at all times and wait until you're called in!' I was seated with Frits, Van Drecht and Kramer in the department of softwood. Softwood are all sorts of wood used in construction.

I was thrilled when I arrived home. I had a job! The only thing I had forgotten to ask was how much I would be earning. Work was from 7 a.m. until 6 p.m. Great! No schoolwork to be done among children who were a lot younger than me. No punishment and especially no marks. No, finally I was somebody. My duty was to bring railroad wagons loaded with wood that were waiting at the border, mostly from Czechoslovakia, into the country and quickly figure out how much wood they contained. I was a very good student, caught on quite quickly and got along great with the people in the office. I also connected with the swearing laborers in the yard. My wages were 350 guilders a month. I felt on top of the world, had no worries and at the office they looked up to me.

I, however, had a short temper and didn't know how to deal with negative comments. I loathed any kind of criticism.

Christmas was approaching and the time had arrived for bonuses. They sent me to the post office to get 30.000 guilders. They money was counted in front of me at the window. Although it was done swiftly, I thought I had been able to keep count. Back at the office Van Bruges asked me if everything had gone well. Of course. After a few minutes I was called into the bookkeeper's office. There were ten guilders missing. He wanted me to count as well and sure enough, it was ten guilders short. The director was called in and he, too, wasn't able to come up with the missing ten guilders. This was of course unacceptable. The post office would not be held accountable, which meant it was my fault. How could I have been so stupid?

I thought the criticism very unreasonable and opened my big mouth. 'You should have gone yourself,' I told Van Bruges. He didn't take it well. 'If you speak like that one more time, you're gone, Muller.' I was not going to take this. I threw my things on the desk, got my coat and walked out the door. I was not going to have anybody tell me what to do. Who did they think they were? I slammed the door behind me, got on my bike and sprinted home. Completely distressed I arrived in Biesboschstraat.

What happened? They accused me of stealing ten guilders. I was not going to take that, of course. I should not have done that, just run off. 'Be happy that they taught you a lot.' 'Go back and apologize.' No way. Shortly after the doorbell rang. My mother went to open the door and returned with Mr. Van Bruggen. He thought it was terrible the way I had reacted and walked off the job. They would have been responsible if something had happened to me. After a good cry, I calmed down again. We resolved everything. The following morning I happily returned to work.

48 WRITING POEMS

I would read a lot in my spare time. And I started writing poems. I would fill whole sheets of paper, with many different writings. One poem I kept repeating, even in my sleep I would hear it; I couldn't distance myself from it. It once got an honorable mention. Every day I register the sentences again, shortly and incisively:

They were standing there
with arms lifted
twenty in a row
they no longer thought of anything
they couldn't any longer
they didn't even know
that in front of their eyes
their wives were being raped
and their children
strangled
with their own clothing
no, they just stood
numb, emaciated

they didn't care
if only they could avoid
the horrendous torture
even their urine was red!
who were 'the' people
who did this to you?
but they couldn't think about this either
because,
with a dull blow
they all
fell in a freshly dug grave
and only the convulsions
were an indication to the Nazi men
that these were creatures
that once were alive.

The following poem was also read from time to time:

As fierce as lightning
shoots through the black sky
screams the voice of the deadly
wounded woman
she calls for mercy,
while her traitors
ruin her young body.
Why does this young woman scream
for mercy?
she hasn't done anything
like all those people
but her attackers are cruel
too cruel
she can no longer stand this

and with one look, that cannot
betray anymore, though with a voice, that
cries one word
the last thing she could say
to the Nazi men
this girl screams
'why all of this?'
and the only answer
of millions of voices
at the same time
'Befehl ist Befehl'!

The incident with the ten guilders led my parents to believe that I wasn't suited to be an employee. I would be better off being my own boss.

'It's better to be a small boss than a big servant,' my mother would always say.

So I was tested again. 'Something to do with people,' was supposed to be my calling. At least, that's what the test said. But what would be the best? Becoming a doctor was not an option, given my level of education. Van Manen had given me a certificate that was equal to four years of high school and I had passed on to the fifth grade, but what were you to do with that?

After searching a long time, I found it: I would become a physiotherapist. That was related to the medical field and you would be working with people.

I was admitted to the Vakschool voor Heilgymnastiek en Massage in Kerkstraat in Amsterdam. I did an evening course that lasted three years, with lessons four nights a week.

49 PHYSIOTHERAPIST!

I left Ambachtsheer at six o'clock, at the same time evening classes were starting. It was a race against the clock. I always arrived just a little too late, but they understood my problem. The medical subjects were taught by Dr. Eckhardt, a wonderful man. He explained everything in a calm, relaxed way and every night we listened breathlessly. Jan Rodenburg, the son of a well-known therapist and the masseur of the soccer club Ajax taught us massage techniques. I was very interested in the medical subjects, even though I had to study very hard to get a grip on all the Latin names. Massage was a revelation for me. It suited me very well; every move was easy. I was so good at it that during my second year, I was allowed to teach massage lessons to first-year students. I had no time left for anything else. It was work and study. At home I had them quiz me. Either my mother or Karel were helping me, even on the weekends. And I passed every exam.

The doctors suggested I should take up sport. I tried to join the rowing club De Amstel. They asked me every question in the book but I wasn't worried about being rejected. After all my massage teacher was a member of the election committee. Still, they refused me. 'Salo,' they said, 'with your background we deem it better that you become a member of the Jewish rowing club Poseidon.' I returned home distraught. How was it possible that I couldn't pick which rowing club to join myself?

The friendship between Rodenburg and me was never the same after that. But then after all, the hockey club Amsterdam had also rejected me.

It was during my third year that Rodenburg asked me if I would like to watch Ajax play. It was music to my ears. It would also mean a complete turnaround in my life.

I was doing so well as a masseur that Rodenburg wanted to have me as his assistant at Ajax. He was planning to retire because he no longer enjoyed his job; the boys were getting too difficult to handle. I agreed for the sum of 250 guilders per quarter, although I probably would have done it for free!

Soon I would learn the ropes as well as how to handle boys that were admired by the public. They were stars. I loved it. My health also improved thanks to Drs. Den Doorn, de Jong and Joop Stork. However, I remained nervous and took medication for it. Two puffs a day kept the asthma attacks pretty much under control which, by the way, is a regime I maintain to this day. I had stopped smoking at this point.

My new work with Ajax and my studies made it almost impossible to hold down a day job. I almost fell asleep when, at night, I walked into the warm classroom from the cold air outside. My parents agreed to give notice to Ambachtsheer. They tried their best to keep me, but I saw a different future for myself.

The day of my final exams had arrived. The asthma attacks had worsened because of my anxiety. I failed. I don't think I ever felt as low as at that moment. At home they didn't know what to do either. But they were able to lift my spirits. Everybody fails every once in a while, there's nothing wrong. Just keep going!

I continued studying, which was a lot easier now that I had time during the day to do it. I also did an internship at the revalidation center De Hoogstraat in Leersum, with Teun Andeweg, a great teacher who became a friend. I thought the work was fascinating. I treated people who had survived car crashes, among other tasks. They called me the 'torturer', because I was hard on them. After a year my studies were over. I don't think I've ever had such a good and interesting time working as I did in Leersum.

I took the final exam again. Again I was very anxious and needed extra inhalations. At the end of the day, eleven of the thirteen candidates were called in. My classmate Marc and I were told to wait. We didn't know what to do with ourselves. Had I failed again? We ended up hearing that we were the only two that did pass the exam. And they gave me the highest grade for massage! No one could comprehend how happy I was, after everything. I was on cloud nine.

50 MY TIME WITH AFC AJAX

From that day forward things with Ajax got even better. Jan Rodenburg became tired of working every evening and Sundays, so he resigned and asked me to stay. The boys and even the management were pleased with my work. And thus, during the 1959-1960 season, I became the physiotherapist of the famous soccer club Ajax.

I signed a contract worth six thousand guilders per year. This meant, however, a forty-hour workweek, treating all injured players with support of Dr. Postuma, the club doctor. He also worked for the Boxing Federation and through him I began to treat boxers as well.

When I started at Ajax I was assigned an empty examination room with a single wooden table with a horse blanket in the center. That was it.

When, after passing my exams, I started working as the club's first physiotherapist I decided to talk to the management. Chairman Melchers agreed to my suggestions and Ajax ended up with the best-equipped examination room in the Netherlands. I worked day and night, but the atmosphere was great. Moreover, I also began to receive my own patients. I had to treat them in between Ajax's training hours, but I was able to manage. In my Renault Ondine I flew from home to the Middenweg and back again. But my passion for Ajax would soon be overshadowed.

At that time I happened to massage a patient every Thursday evening at my home. She had a busy job in the ladies' clothing industry and didn't have time to visit my practice during the day. It was all right with me because I could use some extra money outside of Ajax. Besides, my relationship with Tekla had just ended.

Tekla was a beautiful young woman with red hair who worked at the airport, where she was the buyer for a jeweler. Whenever I had time I would pick her up in the evening. After a while I got to know all the customs and security people. I was allowed to park my car anywhere and could walk to the tax-free stores undisturbed.

Tekla was living with her parents. It was a large family with two beautiful sisters. Once Tekla happened to arrive home late for a birthday party. 'How come you're so late?' her mother asked.

'I went to see the jeweler at Bankrashof in Amstelveen. Their business is not doing well. They may even go bankrupt.'

'That serves her right, that dirty Jewess,' her brother-in-law commented.

It suddenly became very quiet in the room. What would Salo's reaction be? Of course, it was not difficult to guess. I got up, thanked Tekla's mother for the 'pleasant' evening and left.

The next evening I picked up Tekla at the airport. We drove to the restaurant De Bosbaan where we talked. It was our last evening. She never again joined my father to go to an Ajax game on a Sunday afternoon, the way she used to.

51 CONNY

Karel and I went to the Bamboebar in Korte Leidsedwarsstraat, a trendy café with good music. Music was one of my great passions, the reason why I used to go there very often. The doorman Joop, a nice guy, would never let me wait in line. As the masseur for Ajax I had made quite a name for myself.

On this particular Thursday, Aunt Mary, that's what my patient was called, cancelled her appointment. Her cousin from Canada was coming for dinner. I should come on Wednesday instead. During the massage on Wednesday, the doorbell rang. Ru, Aunt Mary's husband, opened the door.

'It's Conny!' he exclaimed.

Conny was the cute cousin from Canada, from Toronto to be exact. She happened to be in the neighborhood and had decided to stop by. She too was employed in the fashion business and would enjoy working in her aunt's store for a while. She was an apprentice fashion designer with her own modest brand named 'Conny's Original'. And there she was, the most beautiful girl I had every laid eyes on: not very tall, slender, dressed according to current fashion and with beautiful hair. My mind began to work feverishly. How was I going to handle this? The moment I had finished washing my hands I knew and I asked her if she maybe would like to go to Noordwijk the next day and spend time on the beach. It was my day off with Ajax so that would work out perfectly. She immediately said yes. She loved the ocean and the beach. As I learned later, she had been a swimming instructor during her summer holidays. She was a sports-loving gal who had taken part in acrobatic swimming and was a superb skater.

The next day we were off to the beach. Everything went according to plan. Sun, no wind and hardly anyone on the beach to disturb us. It was a memorable day, dining at the Landbouw, parading through the shopping area, a herring and afterwards coffee and a waffle with whipped cream. It was what's called love at first sight.

Conny had been able to extend her stay for three more months. Her parents in Toronto were not too happy about it but if that's what she wanted to do, she might be able to learn a lot in Aunty Mary's store. And thus Conny was doing her internship, but she didn't earn a penny and had to find a job to support herself. After searching for a long time she found work with the VVV, an interesting job inspecting hotels. In spite of our busy lives, we had a wonderful time, during which we had a chance to get to know each other well. We got engaged on June 13th.

Conny and I had a lot in common, even our war experiences. When she was fifteen months old her parents were arrested. Together they walked to the assault truck at Afrikanerplein with Conny in the baby carriage. They stood there, patiently waiting until they had to get on the truck. Suddenly one of Conny's aunts, Aunt Stella, appeared.

She grabbed the baby carriage and walked away with it. Shortly after her parents were ruthlessly pushed into the truck. They would be transported via Muiderpoortstation and Westerbork directly to the extermination camp Sobibor. Rebecca and Louis van de Sluis were only twenty and twenty-five years old. Aunt Stella would become Conny's mother.

Little Conny went into hiding with Theo and Nien Tromp in Limmen and registered in the marriage register of these courageous people. Theo and Nien had only recently been married and Connie was their first child. Her new parents were very happy with her and she blossomed. She had three more sisters and a brother. Father Theo went into the resistance and mother Nien became a courier to deliver messages to the resistance and hidden Jews.

After the war the same thing happened to Conny that had happened to me. Suddenly the brother of her late mother came on the scene. He came to claim her, but her parents refused. She was, after all, their child and nobody would take her away from them.

But the judge decided differently. Connie had to go with her uncle and aunt. It was a tough situation. For the second time: 'Bye papa and mama, bye brother and sisters!' The parents were heartbroken. So much so that those courageous people emigrated to Rhodesia, presently Zimbabwe.

Although things in Holland were getting better economically, this was not noticeable for the Jewish population. Many who had gone through the ordeal couldn't find rest. Barely supported by the government and the rest of the population, they felt like strangers. They had lost their home and their livelihood was gone. But even worse, their family, father, mother, husband, wife and children, they were all gone. A few held out hope that someone would return from the camps. Only a few were so lucky that a member of the family after long wanderings found a way 'home'.

Conny's foster parents had survived the war, hidden under terrible circumstances, crammed in with lots of people in one room. When her real parents did not return they decided to adopt Conny. She had become part of the family, they thought.

After the war many children were taken away from their foster parents. Few asked themselves if this was the right way to deal with those little children. Many became lost as they were unable to deal with the separation. Judges made decisions without asking themselves what the right thing to do was for these children.

Because of such a judgment Conny ended up with her 'third' set of parents, a grandmother and an aunt. The grandmother, Sara, was the mother of her 'new' mother, Stella Outs, who was married to Arie Cohen. He was the brother of her real mother. They lived with two of Stella's sisters, Wies and Zus.

When Arie Cohen wasn't able to find a job and, on top of that, was refused the a permit to take over the upholstery from his deported family, they decided to emigrate to Canada. Conny had just started school.

She had been able to accept the departure from her little sisters and brother Tromp and even gained a few more friends. Then right when she started to enjoy things agains, the biggest shock of her life came.

She had to leave again, but this time far away, to a far and distant country where nobody could understand you: Canada. Before she knew it, everybody was standing on the pier in Rotterdam, crying. From there the ship *SS Amsterdam* left, away from everything and everybody, bound for the unknown. Weeks later she arrived in Toronto where friends welcomed her, Mau Coopman and his wife Til.

They moved into a small apartment with little furniture, since they didn't have very much after all. Those were difficult times. Her parents had to work hard and Conny went to school. This wasn't easy for a child that didn't speak English, but the situation improved gradually. Her father got a job as an upholsterer and her mother found work as a seamstress in a factory.

Conny turned out to be a good student. After finishing high school she began her studies in fashion design at the Ryerson Institute. The situation of her parents began to improve. Arie earned enough and thus Stella decided to stay home. Finally things had started to look up. They made many friends, Conny through the Institute and her parents through the Dutch Club. Their friends were all immigrants. But still, the wounds from the war didn't want to heal, especially not where it concerned her mother. She missed her mother and sisters in Amsterdam. But to return to Holland was not an option. It was too expensive and they didn't have that kind of money.

Conny began to design her own clothes and her own brand 'Conny's Original' began to take shape. Being the pretty girl she was, she was chosen as Miss Ryerson. She had turned into a real Canadian.

Her parents tried to adjust as well, except Stella wasn't doing too well. She was overly worried about anything and everything and if something didn't go quite right, she became anxious, a leftover from the war years. This condition would stay with her all through her life and eventually turned into obsession.

During her final year at Ryerson Conny had to do an internship. It was best for her to do that in Holland with 'Aunt' Mary – she worked at Van Duuren in the ladies' fashion industry after all. Another benefit was getting away from her parents and not having to perform, at least for a while. Conny was looking forward to it.

And thus, on a beautiful day, she flew with KLM to Amsterdam. On the plane she met a girl named Nancy, who also lived in Toronto and was on her way to visit her family in Amsterdam. They decided to keep in touch to exchange their experiences. Conny stayed with grandmother and her aunts at Afrikaner Square. She was shocked by the differences to Toronto. No central heating, no refrigerator, no sinks with warm and cold water in the bedroom, not even a television. Everything seemed smaller, even the stores.

One Wednesday night she planned to visit Nancy, but she wasn't home. Instead she decided to visit Aunt Mary, although she wasn't expected there until Thursday evening. That visit would change her life forever, because that's where she met me. Three months later we were engaged.

Her parents weren't too happy about it but Aunt Mary had only good things to say about me. However, she had made up a list with names of nice guys with whom she wouldn't mind Conny going out. Salo was not on the list. Ju and Louis weren't jumping with joy either. 'You just started to work for yourself, which means you have to work hard. And now suddenly there's a girl. What do you know about her? And she's from Canada of all places? Do you realize what you're doing?'

But I was on top of the world.

We saw each other as often as possible without neglecting my work. Every evening I worked with Ajax until about eleven o'clock and after that I would spend an hour or so with Conny, but always under the watchful eye of her grandmother Saar. When, on Saturday evening, we were going out on a date and we stayed in the car for a while, talking, grandmother Saar, dressed in her housecoat and a hairnet covering her head, would come downstairs. 'What do you think the neighbors will say?'

After three months Conny returned to Toronto with a large bouquet of red roses. We wrote each other every day. Every night I took my letter to the airport so it would be in the last post of KLM. When she arrived in Toronto Conny decided not to finish her studies. She wanted to go back to Amsterdam.

After a horrible flight, the plane had to change its destination to Munich. She arrived in the middle of the night by bus at Museumplein. A quick reunion and thus a quick wedding, we figured. The wedding had to be postponed, however, because Conny's father Arie had a serious heart attack.

Finally on October 13, 1963 the moment had arrived. Conny stole the show with her wedding dress that she had designed and made herself. We were on the front page of various newspapers. It was a beautiful Sunday, Ajax was not playing and almost all players had joined the festivities along with Chairman Melchers. It was a real fairy tale. The wedding took place in the synagogue in Jacob

Obrechtstraat. Our witnesses were my friend Karel de Wolf and Conny's best friend Marjan Coopman from Toronto.

It was a very emotional event. Everybody was thinking about the family members that had been killed and Conny and I were especially thinking about our parents. How thrilled would they have been if they could have witnessed this day? The party afterwards was held in the pavilion of the ICC in Vondelpark.

Initially things weren't all that easy. Conny was very nervous. The first day in our home at Van Breestraat she fainted. Dr. Levie figured it was nerves and slowly but surely we began to find our way. I was getting more and more patients and Conny began to assist me. Meanwhile she kept designing her own clothes and still found time for her big hobby: drawing and painting.

I had a wonderful time working for Ajax. I took care of all the players on my own: the first and second team, the amateurs, the little leaguers and everybody who needed me. I was a talker, a listener and an attendant in the broadest sense of the word. I worked about forty hours a week for Ajax and my love for the club was so intense that I didn't worry about the money. Neither did management, however. They thought things were going just fine.

The only one that thought differently was my new auditor, Jan Mooy. Jan was an ardent and faithful Ajax fan. He owned the largest collection of magazines featuring Ajax that had ever been assembled. He thought my wages, however, were a joke considering the work and hours I had to put in. In their glory days I worked about forty-five hours a week for them, went away every weekend with the first team, joined them during the Euro Cup games as well as at their weekly training camps. All of this for 25.000 guilders per year. I was a married man, who in the meantime had become the father of two wonderful children: a girl, Helen, and a boy, Leo.

We moved from Van Breestraat to De Lairessestraat. My father and his neighbor, Mr. Van Lunnen, assisted a little to turn the home into a dream. Things were going great except for my income. There was nothing left after all the bills were paid. Besides, it was about time for a vacation, which had not been possible the last fifteen years.

Meanwhile, my private practice began to grow. I commuted back and forth between Ajax and my home. The first patients arrived at seven thirty in the morning. I treated patients until ten o'clock. That was actually the time I had to be at Ajax again. It took me exactly eight minutes by car. I always ended up a little late. At one o'clock I would arrive back home to then continue massaging at Ajax at precisely three thirty. At five fifteen I would be receiving my patients at home again. Then a quick bite to eat and hugging the kids and the injured players would be waiting for me in the stadium at seven thirty. These were not only the Ajax players, for other Amsterdam clubs would send their players to me. If nothing unexpected happened I would be home between eleven and twelve thirty. For fourteen years I was able to continue this mode of operation until Jan Mooy intervened at last.

He and I made up a short wishlist with the help of Dr. Rolink. An assistant for the massages, not having to attend every regular game with the exception of the first team and compensation for expenses. Altogether not very large demands from a club like Ajax, one would think.

After days of deliberation the chairman, Jaap van Praag, finally addressed my list. 'Salo, you are our mascot, our Mr. Ajax. The way things were going was perfect. Unfortunately we are not able to meet your requests.' How was this possible?

In the end, the evildoer seemed to be the man who had kept me going by prescribing antibiotics and painkillers for recurrent stomachaches due to having made the wrong diagnosis. Rolink thought that I had a real 'smausche' (Jewish) stomach! Later it turned out that my appendix was in fact crushed. My teacher and godfather, Hans Tetzner, had to take it out with some kind of small vacuum cleaner. I could easily have died.

The Ajax management stood behind Dr. Rolink, after all he knew what he was talking about, even though he showed up at the games only about once a week for half an hour and on Sundays. He didn't seem to see the necessity for an assistant. 'Salo will be able to do it by himself.'

If I wanted to make more money, I had to make a choice. Either keep working for my club for practically nothing or expand my own practice. I chose for the latter.

That's when I learned what made the Ajax management tick. In those days we didn't know the word 'bobos', but they were real bobos!

They were very surprised at my decision, and became really angry. I was no longer allowed to come to Middenweg and within 24 hours I had to return club uniforms, shoes and keys. Secretary Westrik told my by telephone that there would be no more Ajax games for me. Other management members joined in the sudden witch-hunt. Salo was declared dead. Yet, Jaap van Praag tried it on in a sneaky way: 'We will not tell anybody if you take care of our injured players at home. After all you are the best and the way things are going now is not working. Rolink is supporting my initiative.'

I thought this was a choetzpah. I didn't allow them to trick me into it. My Ajax time was over for good.

Still, I had a difficult time coming to terms with what had happened. For example I had to change my whole work rhythm, no running back and forth and not having to massage about twenty players each and every day. I had problems sleeping and had reached a state of limbo. No training camp, none of that any longer. Asthma and stomach problems began to create issues again. I had to take all kinds of calming medication, but my many health problems began to scare me. I turned into a hypochondriac of sorts.

We decided to take a vacation to Knokke in Belgium, a beautiful city. It had a friendly population and a beautiful beach and the food was delicious. But I could not relax here either. I called my family doctor every day and each time he was able to calm me down.

I was glad when we returned home. Weekly visits to internist Stork followed. We had become acquainted during the time that I was still working for Ajax. I had taken him to all sorts of activities. Dr. Stork wasn't able to find anything wrong with me. Still, I felt sick.

In the end, the final diagnosis was a burn-out. The time I spent with Ajax had wiped me out completely and consequently I had to pay the price. To have to work for almost fifteen years continuously without a single day off, what did you expect?

There were other facts playing a part as well. Every time I was watching kids play on the beach in Knokke pictures were brought to mind of parents who, during the war, had had to leave their children behind and I tried to imagine what it must have been like.Those thoughts made me even sicker. It must have been horrible for the children, something many were never able to recover from. If they had even survived the war; many of them were still taken without their parents and murdered.

How about the people who had to live with this, who by now were possibly having children of their own? But life goes on. You accept, voluntarily or involuntarily, your new parents, your caretakers, your new environment.

Many were able to face it but not all. It is not surprising that some of them ended up on the wrong path.

Social workers were (and still are) called in. They were sympathetic young people but what do they know about the grief of war? They got their knowledge from books and hearsay. Even the people at the Pension and Advisory Board don't have a clue. I had registered myself with them and after several interviews explaining all my pain, in 1974 I was admitted as a war victim. To me, they are and always will be bureaucrats without insight or feelings.

I won't bother anyone with the list of questions that my wife, along with a doctor of the Pension and Advisory Board, had to answer. You wouldn't believe it anyway. They determine what will happen, it doesn't matter what you tell them. My lawyer gave up, and another wouldn't even take my case. 'A case against the Pension and Advisory Board? You can't win. Not even we can.' My letters were seldom or never answered. Judgments from the Centrale Raad van Beroep were just ignored. They lack any sense of humanity.

I read somewhere that some victims of the war compare the Pension and Advisory Board to the Jewisch Council. Everything at the Pension and Advisory Board happened behind closed doors. They were an autonomous organization, which is what made them so scary. If you don't agree with a judgment from the Pension and Advisory Board, then you can go to the Centrale Raad van Beroep in Utrecht. All of it was horrible actually. A public hearing where victims of war were supposed to tell their story. Share all of your pain and sorrow. Incomprehensible! With the help of my Dr. Hoonhoudt and Drs. Stork and Goldwasser, I now receive a monthly payment. The Pension and Advisory Board later joined the SVB (Social Insurance Bank) and the situation seems to have improved, fortunately. It's also less busy these days of course; unfortunately many have passed away already.

After processing all of this, I focused on my own practice. It grew to one of the biggest in the Netherlands with the help of Willemien Talsma, Madeleine Philips, Elly van Wijk and many other employees.

Because of my work with Ajax, a lot of people in sports visited my practice, such as Erica Terpstra, Ard Schenk, Peter Post, Anton Geesink, Wim Ruska and many other famous athletes. Slowly but surely other sport clubs and even musicians came to us, among others the Concertgebouworkest, and ballet stars such as Margot Fonteyn, Nureyev, members of the national ballet and the Scapino Ballet. Actors and actresses such as Rex Harrison, members of Toneelgroep Centrum, Josephine van Gasteren, Piet Römer, Ton van

Duinhoven and his wife Ina van Faassen, Johnny Kraaijkamp and Rijk de Gooyer also stopped by. Other famous people included: Joop den Uyl, Jan Franssen, the commissioner of the queen in Zuid-Holland, Rob de Nijs, Ben Cramer, Wim Sonneveld, Seth Gaaikema and Robert Long.

The practice was a cheerful and sometimes playful place. We worked with a lot more people now, among others Sam, Monique, Mieke, Gabriëlle, Jolanda, Marjan and Ciska who all gave their everything to help me run the practice. We were growing and became so big that we had to move. We moved the family along with the practice to southern Amsterdam. Our dog Beauty, a great animal, came with us of course.

Beauty's history is a whole other story. When Ajax had to play in London for the Europa Cup, we stayed in a magnificent hotel, an old castle. There were two sand-colored Labradors walking around and everybody loved them. I joked to the manager that I would like to have one of these dogs.

The same man came to me the next day. He had a dog for me. The head commissioner's wife, who bred these dogs, had reserved one for the English ambassador in Australia. But the ambassador had decided not to go ahead with adopting the dog, because the dog would have had to spend six months in quarantine. If I was able to meet some requirements, I would be allowed to keep the dog. I had to give them my passport, I needed to have a certificate of good conduct faxed over from Amsterdam and they cross-examined me.

What was our family like, was our house suited to a dog and did we have a garden? They asked if the children were good children, and above all, could we take care of a dog?

I passed. After the payment of thirty pounds – ten guilders at the time – I became the owner of Arctos Beautiful, a three-month-old female. She was a beautiful animal, whose grandma was a dog show champion in Europe. Her mother had also won awards. The next morning, right before we took off, Mrs. West walked in with Beauty. She had also brought the puppy's mother. It was an emotional goodbye. Beauty was kissed everywhere and her mother licked her head and I received all sorts of instructions and a diet plan, a box of Kleenex and a bag of vitamin tablets. I had my hands full, so Johan Cruijff took Beauty. Dr. Rolink gave her some Valium, so she would stay calm on the plane. That worked out, because she spent the entire flight asleep.

Conny and the kids were waiting for us. Beauty was so nervous that she peed on the treadmill a few times.

We listened to the instructions and we corresponded with Mrs. West for years. Beauty grew up to be a beautiful dog that was with us for over fifteen years. Unfortunately we had to let her go under bad circumstances. We never adopted another dog. We didn't want to live through such a goodbye again.

In the meantime, how were my parents and sister doing? Tet was married to a Belgian boy, named Ignace, and had two beautiful kids, Bernard and Jacques. They lived in The Hague.

My parents were doing well as well, and we visited them often. When my dad stopped working at 74 years old, things went downhill. My mother didn't tell us about it at first, but by father became forgetful and even aggressive. I couldn't imagine it. Louis, the sweetest, softest, most helpful man that I knew? It turned out to be true. He was confused all the time and had panic attacks. At night in the dark he would panic. My mother would call me and I had to talk him into calming down. He didn't want to wear his socks anymore, he would think that his deceased parents and brothers would visit and would start screaming at my mother.

He couldn't remember anything. Not where he lived, what his birthday was, our birthdays, our names and even the grandchildren's names. He wanted to count his money all the time, or take his handkerchief out of his pocket, pee, comb his hair and eat. My mother and I took him to a series of specialists. 'Symptoms of Alzheimer's, nothing to be done.' It was a horrible time for us, but especially for my mother. She wanted to take care of him herself. 'In sickness and in health.' It became her downfall. She had a heart attack. She started smoking even more and destroyed her already damaged lungs.

Louis had a few cerebral hemorrhages and died in his sleep. He was buried on January 21st, 1985 in the Jewish cemetery in Muiderberg with many in attendance. I was devastated. I had lost my father for the second time in my life. It was a strange idea that I couldn't get used to for a long time.

My mother became ill after the passing of her husband. She started having trouble walking and the smoking gave her all sorts of ailments, like blue hands. She was always cold and in pain. She started displaying symptoms of the illness of Renaud, the smoker's disease. She couldn't stop smoking though. 'I'll die five years earlier,' she would say. The years that followed were very bleak. She spent months in the hospital – it was no way to live. The doctors didn't want to intervene. Around Christmas her condition slightly improved. We couldn't see it, but the doctors did, so she had to go. An acquaintance of Tet, an internist in The Hague, helped us 'place' her in Scheveningen, in a nursing home. It was close to Tet, who had moved with Ignace and the kids to Leidschendam.

She had her own room with a kitchen and bathroom, but she couldn't do anything by herself. Conny and I drove to Scheveningen every day. It was the least we could do for her. Her life was a living hell. The brave woman, who used to help everyone, who cooked for people in the neighborhood, who tutored hundreds of kids, now a woman that couldn't do anything, was broken.

The doctors were able to lengthen her life a little with ozone infusions and a lot of oxygen. We took her outside sometimes in a wheelchair. We dressed her warmly in the fur coat that belonged to the doctor's wife and Conny and I took her to the Kurhaus in

Scheveningen sometimes. We could do that because it was walking distance from the nursing home. But she had lost her will to live – she was a weak and tired bird.

She passed away on February 10th, 1991, at exactly seven thirty. She rested peacefully in her bed, with her hands on her stomach. She wasn't worried anymore. She didn't have to cry anymore. She didn't have to think about her murdered mother and sister. She could finally rest.

After we had said our goodbyes, I went back to her alone. I talked to her for ten minutes and thanked her for everything she had done for me. And I thought about what she had given up in order to raise me. I told her I hoped that she would meet her husband, mother and sister 'somewhere'. I told her that because I knew that she wanted that so badly.

Oh I lost my mother Juutje as well. There was an enormous void, even though it was a blessing for her. I miss her the most on Yom Kippur. I have a difficult time when we eat at night. It was always her day, with her fish cookies and raisin bread, her organizing and most of all her herring salad! I try to imitate her every year for Conny. Maybe she finds it funny. We do our best.

And what happened to Conny's remaining family?

I can't pass over her father and mother here. They stayed in Toronto after our marriage and it was difficult for them. Their Conny was gone! Her beautiful room was empty, there was no radio playing the latest tunes anymore. No young people coming over. They also thought it was a shame that she hadn't finished her studies. But they were glad that she was so happy now. We took the children to Toronto a few times, a beautiful and clean city, maybe the most beautiful city I've ever seen. We were impressed with life in Canada. Canadians were hard-working people, and it was much quieter and bigger than Holland.

I got to know a lot of people there, among others the physiotherapist for the Maple Leafs, Karl Ellief. He had the same job as I did for Ajax. He just made ten times as much. He had his own office, phone and car with a parking spot. His wife had a reserved spot on the grandstand. For life, no matter what happened.

He suggested I come and work for him. I wanted to, but my bond with Ajax was too strong.

I also couldn't leave my parents. Did I even dare to go? I don't think so. I was always happy to return to Amsterdam.

It was something that the war had done to me. 'Separation anxiety', they call it. It affects me to this day. I still don't enjoy going on vacation. I'm always scared that something will happen, that my asthma will strike up. I always bring all of my doctor's phone numbers and a great collection of medication.

We weren't going to Toronto.

The goodbye was always very emotional. Conny's mother, Stella, was restless and anxious and always had a headache. She had lost brothers and sisters in the war as well. And her daughter and two sisters were far away in the Netherlands. Without her. Arie had a good job in Toronto and made a good amount of money. That wouldn't be possible in Amsterdam. So the homesickness stayed, which affected her greatly. They saved day and night to be able to visit us twice every year. That was always amazing, for the kids especially.

But my father-in-law became ill. It was his heart. The war had left its marks on him as well. He had lost all of his family and had had to start a new life in Canada. First you need to learn the language and as a foreigner you have to work twice as hard. If people weren't satisfied, they easily fired you. His wife's care and the medication helped him a great deal. But he couldn't stop smoking. He would light a cigarette every time he got the chance.

My mother-in-law visited Amsterdam again. Arie would follow a week later. Everyone was happy. Presents for the kids. On a Wednesday, our day off, we went to Noordwijk. However, Stella couldn't calm down. She wanted to go back to Amsterdam. 'Call Arie and see if everything is alright.' She couldn't get a hold of him. He must have been working.

At four o'clock his good friend Mau called. Arie had called him because he had trouble breathing. They had given him oxygen and he was admitted to the hospital. Mau called back later. Everyone was panicking. 'I wish I hadn't come to the Netherlands alone. If I had stayed home, nothing would have happened.' Stella was desperate.

The phone rang again. I answered. 'Arie has just passed away as the result of a pulmonary embolism.' It was July, 1974. It was an enormous shock. Stella collapsed and Dr. Stork had to come by and give her an injection.

Everything was like in a dream. We arranged a passport for Aunt Zus and she travelled with her sister to Toronto. Arie was cremated there, and his ashes were scattered at sea. 'His ashes might blow over to Holland,' they said.

My mother-in-law was never the same again. She always blamed herself for coming to Holland early.

Grandma Saar, her mother, was suffering from dementia. We visited her as often as possible too. She would see people walking on the roof and was afraid for the children. Arie was her favorite.

'How is he doing?' she asked daily. She had become a brittle, white paper doll. We never told her that her Aar, which is what she called him, had passed away. Arie, who had only lived until 52 years old. Grandma was doing worse and worse. She could barely walk and hobbled around the house. And she was restless. One night she fell from her bed and broke her hip. A few weeks later, on February 10th, 1975, she died in the Boerhaave Kliniek in Amsterdam.

Aunt Zus and her sister Wiesje moved to Buitenveldert, to a beautiful and spacious flat at Van Nijenrodeweg. It was on the eighth floor with a nice view. Every Sunday morning we visited them with Leo and Helen. They always had snacks and the children were allowed to touch everything.

My mother-in-law had moved to Amsterdam in the meantime. After wandering for a while she finally got an apartment in the same building as her sisters. But she wasn't doing well. She met a man, who might have been good for her, but she couldn't forget Arie. It was like she had lost her will to live. She also became diabetic. One Sunday morning her boyfriend Mike called us. 'Your mother-in-law is not doing well.' She was unconscious on the floor. Slowly she came too. The doctor couldn't find anything wrong with her. He thought it was nervousness. It turned out to have been a serious heart attack. She passed away in her sleep on February 18th, 1989 in the intensive care unit. She wanted to be cremated as well.

Wiesje died completely unexpectedly from a pulmonary embolism, in the arms of her sister. Aunt Zus was then my wife's only remaining family member. After her sister's death she was upset, and started having trouble with her heart. She couldn't sleep anymore, alway heard strange noises, imagining it to be music in the neighbor's house. But it was just the sounds of the central heating.

Conny took care of her as well as she could. Her friend Mary – the Aunt Mary who survived Auschwitz – supported her. She called on the morning of December 3rd, 1992: 'Zus isn't doing well, she has trouble breathing.' The doctor couldn't come right away, so we called an ambulance. They tried everything to save her life. She died in the ambulance on the way to the hospital. Conny was driving behind them.

She was cremated privately. She didn't want a grave with a stone either, unfortunately.

Aunt Mary died on May 8th, 2004. She was cremated.

'Now it's just me,' Conny said after the cremation. We suddenly all realised it. And we also realised there was this big void for the kids. There was no family left. No grandpa and grandma, no Zus, no Wies. We thought about the holidays. What would we do now?

Well, at least we have each other!

52 A CLOSE-KNIT FAMILY

We are a very close-knit family. Helen was born on April 17th, 1966, on the same day as her grandma Stella. Leo was born four years later, on January 6th, 1970. What a blessing. Great kids. Maybe they will be the start of a big family.

Helen grew up prosperous. She was always happy, always smiling. She really enjoyed everything. She moved from the Daltonschool to the Openluchtschool, and then to Het Amsterdams Lyceum. She got her secretary diploma from Schoevers. She had good jobs, first at the Hilton Hotel, then at Hotel Krasnapolsky, Maison van den Boer and finally at Egon Zehnder. After a long search, we found a nice apartment for her. It became an open house for many. Everyone came to her with their problems. Even Snoepje, the little cat that just happened to walk in one night. She was allowed to stay.

She met her high school boyfriend Michael Philips, and they got married on May 7th, 2000. It was a beautiful party in the Hilton Amsterdam. Rabbi Soetendorp officiated in the synagogue. At the party, one of the waiters spilled a glass of wine on her wedding dress. Everyone was upset. Not Helen, she thought it was funny. It was typical of her. That's just how she is. Positive. Amazing. After some adjustments, she was able to wear her dress again that night.

Conny and I were, for many reasons, very tense that day. It went by us like a movie. I kept thinking about my parents. Their granddaughter was getting married. If only they could have been there. There was no one from Conny's family. On my side of the family there was Tet with her husband and children and my cousin Aby with his wife. They thought I looked emaciated, I had lost about six kilos because of all of the tension before the wedding. At the end of the night Helen sang a song for Michael. I couldn't keep it in any longer. I started crying. Conny was doing better than I was. Luckily she's less emotional than I am. I should follow her example.

It was a great moment for me and Conny: a beautiful and emotional occasion.

Helen and Michael now live in Buitenveldert, not far from us.

And, what joy! We had a granddaughter. Her name is Rachel and she was born on the 8th of May, 2001. A beautiful, lively child with red hair. A beauty. Then on February 20th of 2004 Benjamin was born, a healthy grandson. Rachel is creative. She draws and she worships her little brother. Benjamin likes sports. He plays soccer in the little league of AFC. Maybe he will one day play for Ajax!

Leo also makes us very happy. We're very proud of him. He also attended the Openluchtschool. Early on he complained about stomachaches. He had a difficult time with his health. The doctors didn't recognize appendicitis. An operation followed with a lot of complications. It was a terrible period for him and for us. Luckily everything turned out OK.

He also went to Het Amsterdams Lyceum and the Maimonides. Despite bad advice from some teachers, especially the ones from the Maimonides, he passed his final exams. Then he went to college. He wanted to become a dentist, and he became one. He's had his own practice all of these years in Maasstraat and lives in a beautiful house in Buitenveldert as well. He has three cute kids. Isa was born on March 21st, 2006, Ava was born on June 16th, 2008 and little David on November 20th, 2010.

The girls both like sports and David wants to be a soccer player when he grows up of course!

Tet and Ignace are grandma and grandpa to three lovely boys. They live in Voorschoten.

Our lives are quieter nowadays.

Conny still paints and she's very good at it. Every once in a while she has an exhibition. She spends a lot of time with the grandchildren. We see them all the time and it's always fun. Grandmas and grandpas are allowed to spoil and aren't responsible for the upbringing!

Sometimes I visit the practice, which was taken over by Madeleine years ago. Snoepje, Helen's little cat, lived with us for years. We had to let her go as well.

Life continues as usual. Thanks to Ajax I became 'a well-known Dutchman'. A Jewish Dutchman. I think the latter worked against me a lot. But I ignore this and continue with my life, with my work and my daily pursuits. I have published a lot and tried to promote physiotherapy as much as possible. I was the editor in chief of *Fysioscoop*, the leading magazine for physiotherapy, for over thirty years. The magazine no longer exists.

I've worked with an acupuncture practitioner for over thirty years. I also advise many colleagues about sports injuries.

In my spare time I listen to music. Sometimes I have my own jazz radio show at Radio Amstelveen. I was the president of the Kiwanis Club for years. I was also the first City Prince of Amsterdam: Prince Salo the First, with the golden hands.

To my great surprise, I received a royal decoration a few years ago. I was declared a Knight of the Order of Orange-Nassau. It was a great honor.

Moreover, I received the Gouden Speld from the mayor of Amsterdam for my work with Ajax and promoting the city of Amsterdam. It is also something to be proud of.

And naturally I go to every game that 'my' Ajax plays on Sundays in Amsterdam.

Once a year I take care of the players of the Money Match. It's a special match between financial managers and financial journalists, a party that has been held yearly since 1974.

Every year we spend some time in Knokke. I write a lot when I'm there. I also wrote my books about Ajax and the practice there: *Mijn Ajax* and *Blootgeven*. In July 2013 my first novel was published.

We enjoy the beach life. We spend time with Sonia, eat ice cream over at Liliane and often eat at Frank van le Siphon in Oostkerke and at restaurant Lispanne in Knokke. We find peace here and can forget many of the horrible things.

EPILOGUE

So what happens next? I follow what is published about Jews meticulously. Most material is against the Jews. There are a few schools and organizations where anti-Semitism is taught. I recently found anti-Semitic quotes in Belgian schoolbooks. As long as a government looks away and doesn't do anything, nothing will change in the mentality of certain people.

Anti-Semitism is rearing its head in the Netherlands as well. According to the Centrum Informatie en Documentatie Israel (CIDI), the increase in anti-Semitic incidents can be attributed to second- and third-generation Arabic youth.

The famous documentary maker Willy Lindner says: 'We still haven't learned anything.' He feels less and less at home in current Dutch society. In Amsterdam Moroccan youths were allowed to disturb the May 4th memorial when Job Cohen was mayor.

The former 'soft' mayor started a dialogue with these kids. They were taught how to commemorate. This mayor was replaced by Eberhart van der Laan. In France the anti-Semitic violence has increased as well. Cemeteries are destroyed and synagogues are vandalized by young Muslims.

In Germany the politicians are arguing about the connection between mass unemployment and the rise of right-wing extremism. A big march of neo-Nazis was organized to commemorate the fact that Dresden was destroyed by the Allies 60 years ago. Dresden is the hometown of the extreme right-wing NPD, a party that crosses the boundaries of a democracy. But the German judges haven't outlawed this party.

We know now looking at history how such a mentality can escalate.

Israel's actions are as bad as Palestine's PR is good. Look at Mrs. Duisenberg and everything she dares to claim. Indoctrination prevents the people from ever knowing the truth. And what about the nonsense of former minister Van Agt?

Millions of people, especially in the Middle East, are taught from birth that Jews should be destroyed. That they're bad people, murderers, want to seize power and other similar nonsense. Such hate has caused six million innocent people to be murdered, including my whole family. Recently the book *Deception* was published, which describes how the Palestinian authorities and the Fatah party deliberate incite hatred against Israel. They pay terrorists and anti-Semitic TV shows are aired, aimed at grown-ups and children.

Spurred on by the Germans a lot of fellow citizens contributed to the atrocities that took place during the war. Indoctrination played a big role here as well. Seventy years ago Auschwitz was liberated. Many attended the memorial. Have we learned anything since? I have my doubts. Right before another Auschwitz memorial the World Jewish Congress convened in Brussels. Anti-Semitism was top of the agenda. 'We're really worried about the increase of threats in western Europe,' said the president Cobi Benatoff in his opening statement.

'The rise of extreme groups, radical muslims and an increase in violence are the cause of a growing feeling of insecurity for the Jews in Europe,' said Benatoff, who thinks that there's not enough being done to solve this problem. 'It's being ignored and even spurred on by EU investigations where Israel is painted as a threat to the world peace.' He ended by saying Jews should be able to proudly go out and should be able to take the subway and their kids should be able to go to school without feeling scared. 'We can't allow that Jews would have to hide again.' That's why the president is so disappointed that Ajax recently decided to no longer publicly call itself a 'Jewish' club. It was a stupid decision, because that's what we're fighting against. If we allow our identity to fade, we have failed.

Recently Bolkestein said that Jews should move to Israel if they don't feel safe in the Netherlands anymore. A strange remark. Every citizen should feel safe in the Netherlands. The government is supposed to take care of that.

Let's hope along with Shimon Peres of Israel that peace will soon come to the Middle East. He thinks it's possible. It would work out well for everyone.

GLOSSARY

Het Apeldoornsche Bos

Het Apeldoornsche Bos was a Jewish psychiatric institute situated in Apeldoorn from 1909 until 1943. In October of 1941, 1.549 Jewish patients were registered. In 1943, all patients, doctors and nurses were transported to either Auschwitz or Sobibor. When they arrived, they were murdered immediately.

Adjacent to Het Apeldoornsche Bos was the Paedagogium Achisomag (where they supported my brother), which took in Jewish kids with 'behavioral difficulties'. They also treated differently-abled children. They were all taken to the camps and murdered as well.

Der Anschluss

The annexing of Austria by Nazi Germany.

Aryan declaration

People had to submit this declaration during the Second World War to show that they were not Jewish. In October of 1940 it became mandatory for all government staff and teachers. They also had to disclose if their parents or grandparents were of Jewish decent, as well as note down the ancestry of their partners. All in all, 200.000 people were forced to submit Aryan declarations. Only a handful refused!

Aus der Fünten, Ferdinand Hugo (1909-1989)

This German war criminal joined the SS in 1935. In the SS he became involved in the deportation of Dutch Jews to the extermination camps. In 1941 he was promoted to Hauptsturmführer and put in charge of the office responsible for carrying out the deportations: the Zentralstelle für jüdische Auswanderung (Central Bureau for Jewish Emigration). After the war he was sentenced to life in prison. Originally he was sentenced to death, but Queen Juliana refused to sign the order. He was held in the Koepelgevangenis in Breda, serving his time with Franz Fischer, Joseph Kotälla and Willy Lages. On January 27th, 1989 he was released. He was then 79 years old.

Christiansen, Franz-Friedrich (1879-1972)

Christiansen was the commander-in-chief of the German army in the Netherlands. He was involved in many of the roundups, the biggest one taking place in the village of Putten. He was sentenced to twelve years in prison, but was released after only serving four.

Dachau Concentration Camp

The concentration camp in Dachau operated from 1933 until 1945. Prisoners from over thirty different countries were housed here, and many died because of the poor conditions. A great number of Dutchmen were imprisoned at Dachau for resisting the occupation.

Dolle Dinsdag (Mad Tuesday)

Tuesday, September 5th, 1944. On this day madness swept the country due to a false report from Prime Minister Gerbrandy, stating that the Netherlands would soon be liberated from the German occupier. Panic spread among the Germans. It was not until May 5th, 1945 that the Netherlands was in fact liberated, having suffered through a winter of cold and starvation.

Drachtstercompagnie

A village in Friesland with presently 1.200 inhabitants.

The German Reichstag

The name of the German parliament in the years 1867-1945. It's made up of the words Reich (empire) and Tag (congress). It was replaced by the German Bundestag in 1949.

Eichmann, Adolf (1906-1962)

A German official who worked for SS leader Heinrich Himmler for eight years and rose to SS Obersturmbannführer. He was responsible for the logistics of the transporting of millions of people, in particular Jews, to the extermination camps. In 1961, he was kidnapped from Argentina and taken to Israel, where he was put on trial and executed.

Fischer, Franz (1901-1989)

An SS Sturmbannführer and a fanatical pursuer of the Jews,

commonly called the 'Judenfischer' (fisherman of Jews). After the war he was sentenced to death, but the sentence was later overturned to life in prison. He did his time in the Koepelgevangenis in Breda.

Gestapo

An abbreviation of Geheime Staatspolizei (the German Secret Police) in Nazi Germany. The Gestapo was founded by Hermann Göring, and later it was taken over by Himmler.

Goebbels, Joseph (1897-1945)

A German politician. He had polio at a young age, which gave him a limp. In 1925 Goebbels joined the NSDAP, Hitler's party, becoming head of the propaganda department. His speeches and propaganda movies are infamous. On May 1st, 1945, the day after Hitler's suicide, Goebbels took the lives of his wife, children and himself.

Goering, Hermann Wilhelm (1893-1946)

One of the most important German political and military leaders during the Hitler regime. He was the founder of the Gestapo and one of the most powerful figures in the Nazi Party.

Grebbelinie

The Grebbelinie was part of the Hollandse Waterlinie, a Dutch defense line based on intentional flooding of a particular territory. It ran from Gilders Vallei of Neder-Rijn at Grebbeberg in Rhenen to Zuiderzee (IJsselmeer).

Grüne Polizei

The uniformed police force under the Nazis. The name stems from their green uniforms.

The Hamburger

The *Hamburger Fremdenblatt* was a newspaper in Hamburg.

Hess, Rudolf Walter Richard (1894-1987)

A German politician who was close to Hitler. As Hitler's secretary he helped him write *Mein Kampf*. On May 10th, 1941 Hess flew a Messerschmidt (German bomber) by himself to Glasgow. He was arrested and locked up in the infamous Spandau prison in Berlin. On August 17th, 1987 he was found dead, hanging from a cable. Was it suicide? We will never know.

The Hollandsche Schouwburg

Before deportation, Jews who were arrested in Amsterdam were brought together by the SS in the Hollandsche Schouwburg (Dutch Theater). The building was erected in 1892 at Plantage Middenlaan as a 'house for culture and relaxation'. It was located in the center of the Jewish neighborhood. In 1962 the Hollandsche Schouwburg became a monument for the victims of Nazi terrorism. Inside the names of families and deported Jews are engraved in the walls.

(Nieuwe) Hollandse Waterlinie

The most important defense line in Dutch history. When the enemy approached, the meadows between Muiden and Biesbosch could be flooded.

The Jewish Council

This council was created by the German occupier in February, 1941. It was a Jewish organization that governed the Jewish community. Initially it was intended to serve only Amsterdam under the name 'Jewish Council of Amsterdam'. Soon, however, its reach extended to the whole country, thanks to it being such an effective tool for the Nazis.

Camp Westerbork

Camp Westerbork was built in 1939 for Jewish refugees from Germany. It was known as a transit camp. From here 107.000 Jews were deported to concentration camps such as Auschwitz, Sobibor, Theresienstadt and Bergen-Belsen. Only 5.000 of them survived. A total of 93 departed trains from Westerbork. Since 1983 the camp has been converted into a visitor center.

Kapo

A Kapo was a prisoner in a concentration camp who was supposed to watch the other prisoners. Kapos were often criminals who received a shorter sentence for carrying out these duties. Kapo is derived from the Italian *capo*, which means 'chief' or 'superintendent'.

Kotälla, Joseph (1908-1979)

Head of administration and replacement camp commander in Amersfoort. He was repeatedly treated for mental illness, and one of the most notorious camp commanders; they called him the 'Brute of Amersfoort'. He was sentenced to death by firing squad, but eventually ended up with life in prison. He died in 1979 in the Koepelgevangenis in Breda.

Kristallnacht

An anti-Jewish pogrom in Nazi Germany organized by Goebbels in response to the murder of German diplomat Ernst vom Rath by a Jewish student. On November 9th and 10th, 1938, 91 Jews were murdered, and about 30.000 were arrested and sent to concentration camps. 267 synagogues were destroyed and thousands of stores and homes ransacked, set on fire or destroyed.

Lages, Willy Paul Franz (1901-1971)

During the war Lages was a SS Sturmbannführer and head of the SD (Sicherheitsdienst), the security service of Nazi Germany in Amsterdam. He was appointed as the head of the Zentralstelle für Jüdische Auswanderung (Central Office for Jewish Emigration) in 1941, and was thus responsible for the deportation of Jews from the Netherlands. He was also involved in the arrest and execution of Johannes Post and Hannie Schaft. After the war he was sentenced to death. Queen Juliana twice refused to sign the sentence, so he ended up with being imprisoned for life in Breda. Lages was admitted to the hospital in Vught on May 18th, 1966 with a serious illness. On June 9th the Minister of Justice Ivo Samkalden granted him leave from his sentence on humanitarian grounds. He was even allowed to travel to Germany to have surgery. But according to German law it wasn't possible to extradite him back to the Netherlands. He lived for five more years. In 1971 he passed away at 69 years old as the result of a brain tumor.

Lippmann, Rosenthal & Co.

A German bank, specifically founded to plunder and register Jewish property. Known as the Liro bank, its headquarters in Amsterdam could be found in Sarphatistraat. Karl Mulisch, the father of Harry Mulisch, was the director.

Mussert, Anton (1894-1946)

An engineer, politician and leader of the NSB. He was also the 'leader' of the Dutch people. He was executed after the war.

De Nationale Vergadering

The Eerste Nationale Vergadering (First National Congress) was active in the period of the 1st of March, 1796 until August 31st, 1797, at the time of the Batavian Republic. It had 126 members. The goal was to unite Gewesten and draft a constitution.

Nuremburg Laws

Also called the Race Laws of Nuremburg, or the Anti-Jewish Race Laws, they consist of three racist laws that were instated on the 15th of September, 1935. These laws prohibited Germans from marrying a Jew, and civil rights were taken from German Jews. The Nazis tried to make life difficult for the Jews, in the hope that they would leave voluntarily. These laws paved the way for the Holocaust. The Citizen Law protected the German blood and honor in the interest of 'genetic health'.

NSB

The Nationaal Socialistische Beweging (National Socialist Movement), a collaboration party. The members had the same ideology as the Nazis. The leader was Anton Mussert.

De Peel

A large peat moor area that has largely disappeared. It was situated on the border of the provinces of Noord-Brabant and Limburg.

Oude Schans

People also speak of Oudeschans. Originally it was called 'Nieuwe Gracht' (New Canal), and is a wide canal in the center of Amsterdam.

Rauter, Hanns Albin (1895-1949)

Born in Austria, he was sent to the Netherlands during the war. He became the top SS officer there and head of the police and Commissioner General of Public Safety. He was responsible for the many deaths and the brutality many suffered at the hands of the SS and the police. He was executed after the war.

Rost van Tonningen, Meinoud Marinus (1894-1945)

Born in Soerabaja, he studied law in Leiden. In 1936 he became a member of the fascist NSB party. He was the editor of the *Nationale Dagblad*, the NSB party paper. During the occupation he was named Secretary General of Finance. He was arrested after the war and committed suicide in prison in Scheveningen.

Seyss-Inquart, Arthur (1892-1946)

Born as Arthur Zajtich, he was an Austrian lawyer and Nazi politician. Originally he belonged to the moderate branch of the Austrian Nazis, but turned into a fanatic in the Netherlands. Because of his limp, he was called 'Zes en een kwart'. In 1940 he became Rijkscommissaris in the occupied Netherlands. He was responsible for the deportation of thousands of Jews and the labour participation for the German industry. He lived on the estate Clingendael in

Wassenaar. After the war he was sentenced to death in Nuremberg, together with 22 others. He was hanged in 1946.

Sicherheitspolizei (SiPo)

These were the German police, the SS police service responsible for tracking down and pursuing political and racial enemies of Germany. The most important division was the Gestapo.

SS

Originally called the Waffen-SS, it was a paramilitary organization that later became part of the German army. SS is an abbreviation for Schutzstaffel. The SS was founded in 1925 and was led by Himmler; initially they were the personal security guards of Hitler.

Süskind, Walter (1906-1945)

Born in Germany to Dutch parents. During the war he was appointed by the occupier as the Director of the Jewish Council in the Hollandsche Schouwburg. He was able to manipulate the personal information of many children and managed to save more than a thousand babies during the war from the daycare across the street from the Hollandsche Schouwburg. He knew Aus der Fünten from his school years.

Ureterp

A village in the Dutch northern province of Friesland with about 4.750 inhabitants.

VAMI (Vereenigde Amsterdamsche Melkinrichtingen)

A milk and ice-cream factory. One of the drivers, Ome Co, was my first host when I went into hiding.

Wehrmacht

Also called Deutsche Wehrmacht. It was the name for the German army as it developed during 1935-1945 under Hitler's leadership in Nazi Germany.

Made in the USA
Columbia, SC
01 April 2024

33860974R00109